NORTH NORWAY

Seasons of Sun and Snow

Edited by Ben Mervis
Photography by Liz Seabrook
Illustrations by Anine Hansen

FARE
FOLK

The Land

The Light

The Living

6	Introduction
8	The Trumpet of Nordland
10	The Dream of North Norway
14	In the Sea, On the Land, In the Hand
18	Light and Colour in the North
34	The Geology of North Norway
36	The Gateway to the North
44	Marianne & Per Einar
88	At the Crossroads
112	The North Cape
120	Journey Up the Helgeland Coast
130	The Natural Household on the Helgeland Coast
136	Wangbrygga
148	Marte & Eric
168	Day and Night
172	Ingrid & Remi
218	Mørketid
228	Henningsvær
242	The Fisherman and the Draug
264	Trevarefabrikken
284	Aligned
290	Kvitnes Gård
318	The Reindeer and the Sámi
320	Máret Rávdná Buljo
364	Childhood Memory of Nordland
366	Acknowledgements

Introduction

BEN MERVIS

North Norway defies expectation and assumption.

It is an area which officially begins in Nordland ("North land") county, but snakes up Norway's long slender coastline more than a thousand kilometres into the Arctic Circle. Officially, it consists of three counties: Nordland, Troms, and Finnmark, but we conceive of it as a cultural and geographical region rooted in centuries of history and human experiences. A place defined by duality and dichotomy: complete darkness and never-ending light; scarcity and abundance; home to outdoor adventure and indoor isolation. But it is, above all these things, a region fundamentally defined by the interwoven relationships between living beings and the landscape they inhabit.

This book is dedicated to those relationships – in particular, the ones we've been lucky enough to witness firsthand. Though I've personally been travelling to this part of Norway for almost a decade now, this book is the culmination of several research trips undertaken with two good friends (Liz Seabrook and Ric Bell, the book's photographer and art director, respectively), and loosely follows the narrative of those journeys through the forests, islands, mountains, towns, and village communities of North Norway.

As we travelled through the region, we were always so warmly received by its locals, and impressed by the affection and respect that they have for their own history and heritage – and the space that they make for it. It is our sincere hope that the pages of this book will reflect all of these things: in the curation of topics, stories, and perspectives, the editorial design, and, of course, the wonderful photographs.

It remains to be said that this book is not a guide to North Norway or adventuring therein. Instead we suggest using it as inspiration for charting your own path through one of the world's most stunning and unique regions.

Bear in mind that while the landscape is often the lure, it's the people that hook you – and will keep you coming back for years.

The Trumpet of Nordland

I am to describe how our Nordland is seen,
With mountains and ocean and shoreline between,
With farms and with attributes many.

I write of the rocks and the peaks up above,
Old, troll-like and grey, with hard snow on the domes,
Of hills and of rivers and valleys;

How farmers a livelihood make here up north,
What food and what drink they set forth on the board,
And many another true feature.

Such writing, if it does not satisfy thirst
Or hunger, may give you a moment of mirth;
What more can this author you promise?

FROM *THE TRUMPET OF NORDLAND* BY PETTER DASS (1647–1707),
TRANSLATED BY THEODORE JORGENSON (1894–1971)

Trompeten av Nordland

I Pennen at føre jeg haver i agt,
Om Nordland, hvorledes det findes udstragt

Med liggende Lotter og Lunder;
Om Klipper at skrive, baad' gammel og graae,
Om Snee, som evindelig ligger derpaa,

Om Bakker, om Elver og fleere;
Hvad Landmanden haver for Næring og Brug,
Hvad Spiise de pleyer at sette paa Dug,

Med anden Omstændighed meere.
Slig Skrifter, om Bugen ey mættes derved,
De Sindet dog nogen Fornøyelighed

Den elskelig Læser kand bringe.

FRA NORDLANDS TROMPET AV PETTER DASS (1647–1707)

The Dream of North Norway

EINAR NIEMI

About one hundred and fifty years ago, a dream was awakened about North Norway as a modern region: that a unified territory should be the driving force towards the central authorities in demanding economic and cultural equality. This dream has only been realised to some extent; today, North Norway is divided into three counties: Nordland, Finnmark, and Troms.

A NORTHERN NORWEGIAN ENVIRONMENT IN THE CAPITAL

North Norway was "invented" at a café table in the country's capital, Kristiania, now Oslo, in 1884 by the Nordland Association, the capital's very first rural community association (later known as the Nordlanders' Association, founded in 1862). The members were largely students, artists, and politicians, several of whom eventually went on to have careers at a national level at the same time as they formed the core troops of Northern Norwegian regionalism, with the aim of building a modern region on a par with the rest of the country. Many of the members came from simple fishing-farming communities and had made their way to the capital via the teacher training school in Tromsø. Tobias Olsen from Rana was the association's first leader, priest, collector of folklore, and "the father of the Nordland Train Line." Elias Blix from Gildeskål, also trained as a priest, became a professor at the university, a minister, and a well-known hymn writer. Another theologian in the circle was Anton Christian Bang from Dønna, the first person in Norway with a doctorate in theology. Like his friend Blix, he became a professor and minister, and ended up as bishop of Oslo. Other later well-known North Norwegian members were the president of the Norwegian Parliament, Sivert Nielsen; Richard With, "the father of the Hurtigruten"; and Ole Olsen, a genius composer and musician who was born in Hammerfest.

Like many other circles of transplanted youths in European capitals in the second half of the nineteenth century, the Northerners in the Norwegian capital dreamed of a new future for the region where they were born. The dream was an alternative solution to the offensive nation-state, where the "province" was often politically neglected while its resources were drained.

INVENTED?

North Norway had of course existed before this evening in 1884, as a geographical area north of Trøndelag.

Despite periods of division between the counties throughout history, there is no doubt that this rural association of Northern Norwegians had a perceived identity and community, created through history, legends, language, and political discussions. On the other hand, the circle noted that there was no common name that could strengthen the regional identity. As stated by Ole Olsen, who was present at the meeting in 1884: "We needed a new and unifying name for the county, one which seemed modern and forward-looking, and which at the same time marked that the region was part of the kingdom." During the discussion, the term "North Norway" came up, and it was adopted.

SYMBOL AND REGION

After the café meeting in 1884, the North Norwegian project was launched, the first regionalism project in Norway.

The main emphasis from then on was placed on various forms of symbols that could strengthen the visibility of North Norway. The most important symbol was the new name, but it took time before it came into common use. Another symbol was Elias Blix's hymn "Childhood Memory from Nordland." The poet Knut Hamsun also allowed himself to be mobilised in favour of the Northern Norwegian project with his "Nordland Cantata," which described North Norway as a forgotten region, but which was now coming to life. In 1912, the Northern Norway Association also founded an award to acknowledge outstanding achievements for the region: the Petter Dass Medal. Many of these measures were financed by the wealthy wholesaler Carl Sundt in Oslo, originally from Lofoten. His telegram address was "North Norway."

KNOWLEDGE AND IDENTITY

During the interwar period, there was a particular emphasis on the dissemination of knowledge about the region and stronger politicisation of regionalism. The establishment of the journal *Håløygminne* in 1919 can be seen as an expression of this initiative. *Håløygminne* was strongly rooted in the "folk high school" environment at Trondenes, near Harstad, led by principal Hans Eidnes. He was also the author of the first overview of Northern Norwegian history, *Nordlands soga i oldtid og millomalder* (1921), later edited and expanded. And in 1922, one of Norway's foremost historians, Professor Halvdan Koht, born and raised in Tromsø, wrote a magnificent article on the history of North Norway in one of the country's leading newspapers, *Verdens Gang*, with an emphasis on the region's place in the nation.

Meanwhile in Oslo, then named Kristiania, the Northern Norwegian mobilisation became increasingly visible with the establishment of North Norway House in 1916, and the new café, Café Nord-Norge, which became a popular North Norwegian meeting place in the city.

A key element in the knowledge building was the demand for separate institutions of learning in North Norway. Admittedly, the region had the country's oldest teacher training school, Tromsø Teachers' College, with roots dating back to the "seminary" at Trondenes, established in 1826. Tromsø Museum had also been established in the first phase of the regional development, but now there were strong demands for a gymnasium, more teacher training colleges, separate regional archives, and more. One outcome was the establishment of a teacher training school at Nesna in 1918, however, several other teacher training schools in North Norway were delayed until after World War II.

The initiative of knowledge building that attracted the most attention was the proposal launched in 1918 by merchant Hans Meyer (from Mo i Rana) for a university in the region, located in Tromsø. The proposal created heated debate because the regional builders argued for the necessity of a regional university in order to obtain the necessary academic expertise in the region. From central political and academic quarters, it was claimed that the periphery was not equipped for such a comprehensive academic boost – there was neither "education" nor cultural capital. At this time, there was only one university in the country, which was located in the capital. The debate is quite reminiscent of the debate that took place before the University of Tromsø finally came into being, adopted by the Norwegian Parliament in 1968.

In this second phase of the regional development, the region had to settle for one institutional initiative on a research level, the Northern Lights Observatory in Tromsø, which was established in 1928. Northern Lights research in the region actually had a history that went back to the French Research expedition around 1840 and the observatory on the mountain peak Haldde in Alta, which functioned for two periods between 1899 and 1927.

During this phase, the press also took it upon themselves to be the mouthpiece for the North Norwegian project. From the 1920s, both of the two largest newspapers in the region, *Lofotposten* and *Nordlys*, referred to themselves as "the newspaper of Northern Norway."

NORTH NORWAY AND THE NATION — "NOW THE CHAINS ARE RATTLING"

In the 1920s and '30s, Northern Norwegian regionalism was seriously drawn into political processes.

During the election to the Norwegian Parliament in 1933, a regional project was included for the first time, that of North Norway. Two years later, the newly elected Prime Minister, Johan Nygaardsvold, declared that "Northern Norway will be built together with the rest of the country," and the Northern Norway Association in Oslo took advantage of the new political attitudes. In 1937, the association organised a grand "Northern Norway evening" in the capital's main hall, the University Aula, where the Prime Minister himself gave the opening speech, with the King and Crown Prince as guests of honour. At the meeting, the Prime Minister described North Norway almost as an autonomous region.

When the Second World War came, North Norway was thus on its way to what has been called an "administrative region" or "front region," i.e. a region which the authorities treated with special political attention. It was thought that regional development should contribute to the building of Norwegian national identity in "the vulnerable border districts" and to buffer against "foreign" influence, the same thinking that had resulted in the assimilationist Norwegianisation policy towards the Indigenous populations of the Sámi and Kven.

INTERLUDE

Despite these developments, the rebuilding of the country after the devastation of the Second World War required almost all economic and political attention, so that there was no room for any direct continuation of the North Norwegian regional construction. In the early 1950s, however, the Northern Norway Plan took over, covering the whole of the region and focusing on modern societal planning based on socio-economic theories and social democratic political ideology concerned with effective economic progress and equality between social classes. However, the plan played down the aspects of regional independence.

THE FOLK SONG AND LOCAL HISTORY

Between 1970 into the 1990s, there was a massive mobilisation of the region's history and culture, which contained both a peripheral rebellion against centralisation and against one-sided socio-economic thinking. During this period, North Norwegian folk singing experienced its heyday, the region finally got its own professional theatre, and local history flourished, while at the same time it was professionalised through its close contact with the University of Tromsø. In this phase, North Norway was largely realised as both an identity region and as an administrative region.

PERIPHERY IN THE PERIPHERY

From 1990 to the present day, there were several early signs of deterioration of the idea of North Norway as a unified region. A new debate arose about regionalisation, inspired by the European Union and the "Europe of regions." This term was a leading slogan in the European Union in the 1980s and '90s which foregrounded regions as one of the most important motors for economic, social and cultural development in Europe. The North Norwegian regionalists were inspired by this model.

In 2017, the Norwegian Parliament adopted a division of the country into regions through the merging of counties. The outcome in North Norway was that the old dream of a unified region was shattered: Nordland stayed a separate region while Finnmark and Troms were merged (effective from 1 January 2020). After new rounds of national debate, parts of the regional reform were reversed, and for North Norway, this meant that Finnmark and Troms again became autonomous counties (effective from 1 January 2024).

Today North Norway is split into three independent *fylker* (counties). Despite being separate, they face the same main challenges for the future. The fishing industry in particular is under threat, due to the increase in regulations on catch quotas of cod and the global competition of fishing in general. The rapid increase of tourism is also an issue, with severe challenges for all types of infrastructure. Climate, too, is a major consideration for the changing landscape, as an increasing number of international tourists in North Norway already today are "climate tourists"; those escaping the summer heat in countries around the Mediterranean Sea. These challenges are already being felt in daily life and work in North Norway.

There is, however, much hope for the future of North Norway; in the nineteenth century it was seen as "the land of the future," and even "Norway's America." Today, the vast landscapes offer space for a wide range of uses, from reindeer husbandry to tourism, so long as the people of the North retain a fair balance between the needs of the different cultures that call this region home.

REFERENCES

Aas, Steinar: Å eg minnest. Regionbyggere
i hovedstaden. Nordlændingernes Forening 1862–2012
(Orkana akademisk forlag: Stamsund 2012).

Niemi, Einar: Regionalism in the North:
the Creation of North Norway, Acta Borealia 2/1993.

Ottar nr 4 2019. Special issue on North Norway,
"Nord-Norge — samlet eller splittet?"

Zachariassen, Ketil: Samiske nasjonale strateger.
Samepolitikk og nasjonsbygging 1900–1940
(ČállidLágádus: Karasjok 2012).

In the Sea, On the Land, In the Hand

PER THEODOR TØRRISSEN

Growing up in a small town nestled in North Norway, my childhood memories are intertwined with the quiet charm of coastal living. My dad was a city boy, and my mum hailed from a small village on the island of Seløya. When I was young, we used to visit my grandparents who still lived in that small village, just as they have done their entire lives. The hour-long drive involved navigating winding roads and taking two ferries, a trip I dreaded as a child prone to car sickness.

My grandad, a tall and reserved man, had been both a fisherman and a farmer – a common practice in North Norway. My grandmother, the undisputed boss of the household, was a firm and robust woman. Their home felt old-fashioned yet picturesque, perched on a small hill with large windows framing views of the vast landscape.

Fish dominated the menu during our visits; whether it was freshly caught saithe, cod, or the occasional halibut, my grandmother's cooking usually featured the bounty of the sea. Boiled potatoes, carrots, flatbread, and bacon accompanied the meals, usually with a rich béchamel sauce or simple melted butter. But what really stood out for me as a kid was the event that followed dinner, when everyone was full. That's when the ritual started, and what might be my first memory of a food experience.

As we sat contentedly at the table, a large seagull would appear outside the big window by the dining table, hovering above the plains. Its raucous calls would summon more seagulls, inciting a frenzy like they were waiting for something to happen. Suddenly my grandmother would get up and collect all the scraps from our meal on a platter, and decisively leave the room. Next thing I knew, she was outside. She would pause for a moment before she put the platter heaped with leftovers on the ground, all this while the large seagulls became more and more frantic, diving in to get their share before it was too late.

My grandmother would come back inside and we would all sit in silence and watch the flock clean the big plate in controlled chaos. The seagulls knew exactly when dinner was being served, and my grandmother could also tell if one of her "regular customers" was missing. Looking back, I sometimes wonder about why she did this. Was it to care for the birds, to make sure they were fed, like an extended family? Or was it just a way to reduce waste? Or maybe it was all staged, just to put on a show for a small, bored city boy.

As an adult I moved to Trondheim, where I worked in busy restaurant kitchens for almost ten years. Despite the fact that we imported pigeons and foie gras from France, truffles from Italy, and seafood from the fresh cold waters of the Norwegian coast, we rarely had the time to think about the ingredients; to really consider how they were produced, issues of animal welfare, the cost and labour of transport, the environmental impact, or the working conditions of the farmers, foragers, and fishermen. It was only when my wife and I decided to move back to my hometown in North Norway and I started to work at the canteen of the local agricultural college that my perspective began to shift. The complete change of pace was stark and unsettling; I told myself I'd give it a year.

What I didn't realise was that with the change of pace came time to reflect. I was working in the biggest agricultural college in North Norway, and I slowly began to see the potential. At the restaurant in Trondheim, we used to get these fancy wooden boxes of small potatoes from France; they had a perfect small shape, but were tasteless and expensive. One day at the canteen I was approached by the manager of the school farm who said they had just picked this year's crop of potatoes from the field and was wondering if I was interested in using some of it for the kitchen. I went to the farm to have a look, and there in a large pile was a tonne of small potatoes, just like the ones we used to get from France. I asked the manager of the farm what they usually did with them. "Animal feed," he said. I was shocked, and I replied, "Then I want them." They were ten times tastier than the potatoes from France, and storage and transport hadn't bruised them. They were also fresh from the soil, and the skin was so thin that you could easily eat them with the skin on. What followed was a time of exploration: understanding food systems, learning about different types of agriculture, and surrounding myself with people who knew more than me about the complex systems that are involved in the process of producing our food.

Without realising it, I became more involved with the true essence of what food is, more than I ever was as a restaurant chef. I soon started to work on all types of projects, trying to stimulate more local food production; building bridges between academia, science and food producers; arranging workshops and travelling to other countries to learn. In doing so I began to understand more about what North Norway had to offer, and working with the local producers of the region made me aware of its unique qualities, particularly its diversity of landscapes and resources.

At the same time as I was slowly discovering my own region, the recruitment to the food industry in Norway was facing difficulties. People didn't want to work as chefs anymore, and we couldn't get the kids to enrol in culinary school. Issues with long hours, low wages, and bad working environments had finally taken their toll. We decided to take action, to communicate the benefits of working in the food industry. At one workshop we did, we had diver and sea-forager Roddie Sloan and chef Magnus Nilsson. After a late-night dinner, I ended up talking to Roddie, and we discussed how we could stimulate recruitment, get more young kids into the industry, and work to promote the region at the same time.

With this conversation lingering in my mind, I returned to Mosjøen, where my friends Marianne and Per Einar were running an authentic and cosy café called Vikgården, focusing on local food traditions. I had studied food culture with Marianne, and I knew her to be a visionary, so it was natural to discuss these ideas with her. Fortunately, she felt the same way, and together we started to develop a plan for a festival celebrating the food of North Norway. We built a team of volunteers: Trond who runs the local wine shop, Espen who works in the bank, Runar who was a teacher, and many more.

In Mosjøen we have a beautiful mountain and a river running past the longest cohesive row of old wooden buildings in North Norway, and we decided that this would be our backdrop for most of our events. We invited a wide range of local, national, and international contributors to do talks, food demos, and to cook lunches and dinners. Our network grew, and soon we started to develop other projects, which eventually led to the establishment of a food resource centre. Over the years we've realised the potential in sharing the cuisine and the food produced in the region by getting to know the farmers and fishermen. Combined with the feedback from our visiting guest chefs, producers, food writers and academics, we have continued to grow and develop.

Thinking back, perhaps this journey was inevitable. My mother tells the story that when I was a kid, there was a fishmonger in the city that we would visit, and that my biggest wish was always to go and see all the fish laid out on the counter – that the fish that we had for dinner actually had an identity fascinated me. When we had fish fingers for dinner, I would ask her. "What's the name of this?" She would of course reply, "Fish fingers." And I would say, in a confident tone, "I know that, but what's it called when it's in the ocean?" That was obviously a far tougher question to answer.

From my curiosity and fascination about my grandmother's seagulls, through my career as a chef, and then revisiting that curiosity and fascination so many years later, I feel lucky to have had the privilege to get to know these passionate people, and discover the qualities that lie in the land and sea of North Norway, and in the hands of the skilled people that live here.

Light and Colour in the North

LIZ SEABROOK

It feels somehow paradoxical to ask a photographer to write about light: look through this book and you'll find my answers. Shards of light from the longest days, and the shortest, caught as if in amber, transmitted from prismatic beams to soft colours on paper. Over nearly four years we visited North Norway six times, across all four seasons.

AUTUMN IN HATTFJELLDAL
As the frost begins to settle around us, we stand transfixed by the night sky. Have there always been this many stars? The soft, peachy band of the Milky Way stretches out above us, and beyond the hills ahead colourless bands of light dance faintly on their newly snow-capped summits. I realise, not for the first time, how few of the constellations I know by name. Staring up, mouths agape, the silence around us in the uninterrupted darkness feels more like hiding out in the safety of a blanket fort than anything eerie. The farm stands almost alone, and yet feels entirely safe.

In the morning, golden September light streams through the gaps in the old lace curtains onto my pillow in the back of the old house. The rest of the house lies silent as I pull back the curtain to find the fields surrounding the farm decorated in a heavy layer of glittering frost. I pull on my clothes and creep through the other two bedrooms to make my way out into the newly bejewelled landscape. The grass crunches loudly as I make my way to the bridge we crossed when we arrived. Now coated uniformly white, it feels a little like the boundary to Narnia, steam rising from the water below, showing that it's warmer than the current air temperature. Dragon's breath billows from my mouth as I crouch to inspect the ice-clad grass a little closer. Everything is magical in the dazzling low sun.

After breakfast, walking through the now-dewy sheep field – followed by a curious bunch of fleecy disciples – I pass through the gate into the woods behind the farm in search of goodies. Under the dappled canopy of the birch trees the gold persists, amplified by the yellow leaves of autumn and, climbing uphill, I search for golden chanterelles covertly camouflaged in the early morning light. At the top of the hill, when I step out of the woods, the land opens up across the Børgefjell National Park. Finding a spot atop a rock of disputable comfort, a gust whips across the landscape, spraying the cloudless blue sky with stars of yellow leaves.

SPRING HEADING NORTH

We boarded the Hurtigruten bound from Trondheim to Tromsø earlier in the day. From one side of the boat, snow-covered mountains slip by, pale against the delicate grey of the overcast sky: subtle, quiet shifts in monochrome. Out to sea, the sky is a deep, inky navy, solid at the horizon line. Above us sits a maelstrom of clouds brewing, tumbling in a wrestling match against themselves. A soft mauve outlines their curves. Where the two sides meet, the grey slants into the deep blue, the darkness seemingly engulfing the serenity of the colourless, featureless cloud. Wind whips around the boat, and here looking out to the vastness of the sea, I feel still. It's hard to allow any terrestrial or internal anxiety or problem to feel so big that it could rock you, when nothing but miles of ocean – and a deep sea ledge below – stretch out in front of you.

When we boarded the boat in Trondheim the hills had been grassy and lush, vibrant with spring blowing in, but now moving further north the landscape has gradually slipped from green to white. At one port, we arrive in a blizzard, the dark clouds from earlier in the day finally blowing in to catch up with us. The sun hasn't set, but almost all of the light is blotted from the sky amidst the storm that rushes around the boat like a snow globe. The only highlights that break the scene are the dull orange pin pricks of house lights shining through the windows of invisible houses on the shore. I step out on deck to take a picture, ears and nose immediately burning as the wind snaps at any exposed flesh. With so little dimension to the light and the old-style buildings of this small harbour town, it's hard to believe that I'm observing something real in front of me and not a tableau painted just beyond the bow of the boat. The resulting image feels the same: in spite of the weather and the dwellings captured, there's an odd lifelessness to the scene.

I'm awoken to bright sunlight streaming through the window in my cabin. The sun waited until we reached the true North to show itself. Everything is dazzling. The bluebird sky meets crystal-white mountain tops, and it feels as though every facet of every atom out on deck is fizzing with light. Even behind my sunglasses, my eyes squint as they're met with the full force of the Arctic sunshine. The wind has dropped, and the air has lost its bite. Coaxed from the lounges inside, people spill out onto deck, blinking blearily. There are no soft edges any more; everything is defined by clean, crisp lines. Even the water's waves, gentle beneath the ship, are cut sharp, casting tiny, razor-like shadows back across themselves. Tromsø begins to appear, first as a run of small houses, then to a crescendo of bridges and rooftops, churches standing proud, perfectly outlined.

MIDSUMMER ON HERØY

You're never far from water in Norway. It cuts into the land, slicing away rock to form islands, allowing the sea to fill the ravines between mountains. Great lakes are locked into the land and rivers wend their way across the country, going softly at times and then crashing with such force that their constant thrum has to be shouted over if you stand too close. Waterfalls tumble down rock faces, etching white tracks into slate grey. On the western isles of North Norway this feels truer than anywhere else, especially standing atop of the island of Herøy. This top on which I stand, I would estimate, stands a mere ten metres above sea level. The roads drop and rise a couple of metres above the waves, and you have the feeling standing on the shore that any particularly overzealous storm might raise the water level so high that these little low lying islands would be swallowed in an instant. And yet, looking around, the jagged outcrops of the Seven Sisters are visible to the East, Dønnamannen looms in the North, and way out to sea Lovund stands proud. It's a landscape of stark contrast: pockets of small flat islands surrounded by staggering tall giants.

The last time we visited Herøy it had been September and the flora had been unremarkable. So much so that thinking back, all I can recall is rock. Rock, road and the sea. The sea was alive with myriad colours – it always is, here – but the land lay dormant. Now, wildflowers have sprung up across the islands, forcing their way through the cracks in the rock, carpeting the island in soft washes of colour. White billows up from fields like a low hanging fog, thickly covering swathes of land, houses rising up from the blousy blooms half-engulfed in the lushness of it all. Buttercups, cow parsley, meadowsweet, red campions, and bog myrtle all vie for your attention, hoping they'll be picked as part of a halo of petals in a midsummer crown. Even on the grey days – and, of course, there are many – the flowers fringe the greyness, keeping the gloom at arm's length. Yes, rain has set in, but it's still midsummer in the Arctic and there's so much joy to be had.

On Midsummer itself, the sun can barely contain its excitement. "It's my day!" It seems to cheer. The day passes easily with hellos and catch ups, and strolls around the islands enjoying the warmth, tapered softly by a gentle breeze. At ten in the evening we slide out to sea, the sky still blue with a subtle band of dusky pink beginning to creep up at the horizon. The water – smooth as a mill pond – sparkles gently about the boat, so inviting that when we're done with a successful round of fishing I can't help but take a midnight dip. Lying back into the clear water, I look up into grey-blue, clouds scattered and turn my face to the now crimson colour at the sky's edge. Time spent in water is always magic to me, listening to the soundscape below the surface, washing off any worries, reconnecting back to the vast ecosystem in which we exist, but this swim feels nigh on holy. The sun has dipped entirely beyond the isolated island of Lovund momentarily and rays spray out from its peak, a beacon aflame in celebration of this sacred calendar day.

WINTER AS FAR NORTH AS YOU CAN GO

Funnelled from Alta along a road deep in the belly of an ice-clad ravine sits the small town of Kautokeino, shrouded in a veil of white. The road, a muddy grey artery of slush from the day's commute, is surrounded by thin veins of silver birches; the only thing breaking the interminable white. There's a complete and perfect stillness to it: not snowing, no sun trying to crack through, no stars appearing as night falls, just snow-blind whiteness.

The morning yawns across the hills, slowly and softly bringing light into the valley. Gazing out of the window from the breakfast table, there's barely any definition in anything that isn't man-made: Earth meets sky in the softest monochrome. Until you're here, the true breadth of shades of white is unknowable. Arctic whites, subtle shifts of light where the sun barely comes out to play. Dull rays refract, altering the colour almost imperceptibly. This is the furthest I've felt from water in Norway. There may be rivers, but they're sealed tight under layers of ice. The sulking light also seems to acknowledge this fact, no longer dancing around us.

Bundled up in a large coat, mittens, and insulated trousers, I grip the sides of the snowmobile as we glide across the open plains, the thrum of the engines muffled by the thick layer of snow beneath us. I love the quiet that snow brings, when the winter air becomes perfectly still and serene, and you sense that it will start falling soon. There's no breeze today, but the speed at which we're travelling causes the air to lick at my cheeks. Only saplings surround us, gingerly poking through their white cover, and when they vanish I realise we must be on a lake, indistinguishable from the rest of the landscape. After twenty minutes we spot them: a herd of reindeer. They should be on the move, but a death among the herders has delayed the migration. Some of the reindeer are near impossible to pick out, blending in with the snow. They remain unfazed by our presence, continuing to delve their velvet-soft muzzles deep into the snow in search of young shoots.

THE END OF THE SEASON

Two winters have passed, and I find myself back in the North, gazing at the western isles of Lofoten on our final trip of the project, quietly watching the clouds drape over the distant peaks. The water where I swam the night before gently laps at the rocks below on this unseasonably warm March day, and the scent of fish drying around Henningsvær subtly wafts in and out. It's nearing midday, but the sky remains overcast. You might expect it to be grey, yet there are delicate washes of soft pink through the clouds, and the sea holds a unique shade of dark, inky turquoise that I've come to associate with the Arctic tides. For all its dramatic scenery, what makes this corner of the globe truly remarkable to me is its understated beauty: the small details and hints of colour you almost have to squint to see. There is a quiet majesty to North Norway – you just have to be still enough to notice it.

Autumn in Hattfjelldal

CHAPTER ONE

The Land

The Geology of North Norway

ERIC RYAN

Geological forces shape the world around us, and few countries have been shaped as visibly as Norway. Snow-capped peaks jut above the picturesque, green fjords, with cascading waterfalls reaching down to pastoral grazing lands – such landscapes are so quintessentially Norwegian that for many they form an important part of Norway's national identity. While the fjord-and-fjell landscape does dot along much of the western and northern coastlines, Norway's coast is also fringed by intricate archipelagos, like the twelve thousand islands of the Helgeland coast, as well as ancient mountain plateaus such as the fourteen-hundred square kilometre Finnmark plateau. Such varied and dramatic natural beauty results from aeons of geological activity, and natural forces unmatched by anything else on planet Earth in both power and scale.

As dramatic as the Norwegian landscape is, the pace of geological change is anything but. Understanding the expanse of geological time can be a challenge, but by compressing the entire 4.6 billion years of Earth's history into a single calendar year, we can begin to wrap our minds around nearly incomprehensible numbers. Norway's oldest rock formed just over 3 billion years ago, or in mid-April of our year. The Cambrian explosion, when organisms on Earth shifted from simple unicellular creatures to more complex lifeforms, took place sometime in November. Dinosaurs, including those who roamed through what is now North Norway, didn't appear until mid-December. Humans finally appeared late in the evening on December 31st, while the first nomads to set foot in North Norway didn't show up until around one minute before midnight on the last day of the year. Much has changed in the geological instant during which humans have roamed the North, but the results of geological events long predating the existence of humans, or even dinosaurs, still shape the world around us.

Critical geological structures formed during major events in Norway's geological history, like during the mountain building collision between North America and Europe. Today, Norway remains a mixture of rocks from North America, a lost ocean (the Iapetus), and the European continental margin, forced together in a Himalayan-like mountain range, and long-since eroded into a series of flatter landscapes. Geological structures like folds, faults, and shear zones which formed deep within Earth's crust during the collision still characterise Norwegian geology. Even today, farm fields in coastal Norway generally lie atop ancient faults, where glacial and sea water erosion created depressions which in turn were filled with fertile, calcium-rich marine sediments ideal for agriculture.

Despite never escaping these ancient structures, the Norway we see today bears little resemblance to the ancient mountain range formed between colliding continents. For starters, Norway has drifted from more tropical latitudes to its current northern position. Most of the country was worn down into an entirely flat plain before the coming and going of numerous ice ages carved the steep, mountainous, and beautiful landscape we see today. The end of the most recent ice age paved the way for nomadic migration, as early peoples moved north at the boundary between ice, land, and sea, surviving in the small zone between ice field and ocean where the geology permitted human existence.

The entirety of human prehistory and history in Norway fits into a geological instant, starting with the melting of the ice some twelve thousand years ago. As the ice receded, humans worked their way north, hunting seal, moose, and reindeer, while fishing and finding shelter on the small sliver of land between the North Atlantic Ocean and a vast expanse of ice stretching towards the east. Continued melting of the ice opened new lands in the south. By 5,000–4,000 B.C. agricultural communities developed on ice-free lands near Oslo, while it would take thousands more years before farming became wide-spread in North Norway. The still-cold, mountainous terrain spurred the development of early skis, while the intricate archipelagos, fjords, rivers, and lakes, carved by ice along ancient geological structures, were stone-age superhighways for early skin boats.

The rugged and mountainous coastline, protected by thousands of islands and sheltered fjords, preempted a sea-faring nation with a knack for the maritime that still exists today. The alpine terrain, devoid of fertile soil due to the preponderance of glaciers and therefore unsuitable for wide-spread farming, encouraged settlers to look elsewhere for better lands, and Vikings were born. At the same time, small settlements popped up in areas of unique geological circumstance, where opportunities for fishing, hunting, and agriculture were most promising. Norway's continued development would follow suit, with raging rivers and dramatic topography eventually facilitating hydropower projects, and geological coincidences leading to mineral deposits ripe for exploitation by early miners.

From the Middle Ages, the export of geological resources generated wealth in Norway. Initially concentrated amongst a select few elite, this wealth would in time be shared with the entire populace. Over the past five hundred years, mining has become widespread in Norway. Mineral deposits abound in the deep roots of the mountain range formed by the collision between North America and Europe, some 300–400 million years ago. Offshore, both in deep sedimentary basins and within fractured zones of the Norwegian continental bedrock, ancient algae and other organisms are now extracted as oil and natural gas. The export of geological wealth, combined with sound egalitarian economic policies – arguably a more unique Norwegian feature than its geology – permitted the development of the modern Norwegian welfare state and, somewhat ironically, gave Norway the means to move beyond its geographical bounds.

Many scientists refer to the planet's most recent time period as the "Anthropocene," i.e. a time period in which humans exert significant, even dominant, geological influence on the world around us. Norway has now built over one thousand kilometres of road tunnel, twenty-two thousand bridges and forty-two hundred dams, even in sparsely populated areas like the North. Not only does this building boom allow us to escape geological constraints in our daily lives, quickly driving over fjords or through entire mountains, but Norwegian culture is changing, too. Local dialects in North Norway, which have been pronounced in both number and variation, are disappearing as physical barriers between communities along fjords or over mountains are removed and populations shift. Unique local delicacies such as *blandaball* and *rødsei*, a reflection of cultural, but also specific geological and natural conditions, are in danger of sharing this fate. Such change is not necessarily a bad thing, but our escape from geological and other barriers of the natural world might have consequences which are hard to predict.

Previous generations of Norwegians migrated en force, as geological circumstances bred apt travellers with little to lose in their dramatic, overcrowded, and at times desolate homeland. Modern Norwegians, and immigrants to the country like me, can only consider ourselves fortunate to be residing in an egalitarian welfare state soaked in oil and other geological fortune. The exploitation of these resources has allowed Norway to escape its own geology, moving into a period where humanity, not nature, is the defining player. All this has happened in the geological blink of an eye, at a time scale smaller than what most geological studies even register; it remains to be seen how long these dramatic changes will last. From a geological perspective, it may all be over in an instant.

The Gateway to the North

Darkness hides Mosjøen like a well-kept secret. Waking here for the first time, having arrived late, exhausted, and without any expectation, I pulled back the curtains of my hotel room window to stare dumbly at the fullness of a sun-lit mountain and a quick-moving fjord-fed river two hundred metres from where I stood.

Sjøgata ("sea street"), the road on which I stayed, is the heart of the old town, full of pastel-hued wood-frame homes and boathouses. The street has a sleepy charm that gives it the feel of an open-air museum, where Bergen-bound merchants might embark at any moment. Here, cafés new and old, antique shops, and galleries cater to locals and intrepid travellers alike.

The "new" Mosjøen extends from this point. It is a town built on industry (formerly fishing, and now aluminium processing), but which has recently undergone a process of rediscovering and re-appreciating its culture, context, and heritage as a gateway of (and into) North Norway.

But rarely do I veer far from Sjøgata, because this is where I find my home in the North: Vikgården. Very few places can feel like home on your first visit, but this is one of them. And in our case, the lights are on, I can smell the coffee, and Marianne is making waffles.

Across the Vefsna River, running along the base of the mountain Øyfjellet, a long walking path takes you past sandy beaches, up a gentle slope through trees and along the coast. The path enjoys the best view of the historic old town with its stretch of beautifully painted homes.

Marianne & Per Einar

Marianne Myrnes Steinrud and Per Einar Steinrud are the owners of Vikgården, a dynamic heritage space which exists in a white-washed corner store on a small intersection of Sjøgata, a historic water-side neighbourhood in Mosjøen. Here they are not only the operators, but also the quintessential hosts: ready to wrap you in a hug, fill your hand with a hot (or strong) drink, and ensure you are fed well and often.

Formerly a café and event space, Vikgården now operates mostly as the spiritual home of ArktiskMat ("Arctic Food"), the Mosjøen-based Nordic food festival, for which Marianne and Per Einar are often hosting and cooking large lunches and dinners from the comfort of their cosy candle-lit rooms. Every evening or event at Vikgården is also a welcome into North Norway, with the space laid out like a charming old tavern, and outfitted with original antiques from the area sourced by Per Einar himself.

Childhood sweethearts with children (and now grandchildren) of their own living locally, they have both individual and collective roots in Mosjøen and throughout the region of Helgeland – from the mountains to the coast – which date back generations.

Yet it is perhaps a couple of hours away, at their remote mountain farm called Eldsmo, where they feel most at home. They have visited the area together since their teenage years, and now lovingly tend to and upkeep an old farmstead set on forested land with open pasture for sheep. There, where time moves at its own pace, they attune themselves to the heart of the North.

PART 1
VIKGÅRDEN

Ben Mervis with
Marianne Myrnes
Steinrud and
Per Einar Steinrud

Vikgården is such a welcoming introduction to the culture and heritage of the North. Was that something you wanted to create from the beginning?

MARIANNE: Vikgården has always been about celebrating the history here. I think that everything that we, Per Einar and I, are doing is based on using the tradition and the culture as much as possible in new ways. It's regenerative: taking what we already have and making a business out of it. It started in 2003, when we bought the place. Per Einar's aunt was married to the guy that was trying to sell it then. His last name was Vík, so that's why we called it Vikgården.

The Vík family had run it for three generations before us. From the beginning, the house was built for trade, you could buy whatever you needed – coffee and oil, and the kinds of things that were in every old store in those days. It wasn't the first trade house in Sjøgata, but it's one of the oldest houses.

It was originally built in 1883. They renovated it in 1897, so since then it has looked the same from the outside. It's an old house with a lot of history and we immediately fell in love with the place. But it didn't look like it does today when we bought it in 2003. We were supposed to buy a place up where we now have Eldsmo [the farm]; that was our dream. We wanted to have a place where we could make food and have guests. But we were waiting for ten years. And then ten years in, we thought we were at an age that we needed to start acting on some of our dreams. That's why we bought this place. And instead of a farm in the mountains it was kind of a city-farm place.

We renovated it for a while, to take it back to what it was originally. We could see what it was like, underneath all the panelling, and we got a young guy to build us new shelves and help us get it back to the original atmosphere.

Over time, with hard work, it has become what it is today. We wanted to own everything by ourselves; we didn't want to have a big loan from the bank so that they could make us do what they wanted us to do. Since we started the business, we wanted to have control and work hard ourselves. We had small children the whole time, so they grew up here and they started working really young and helping out; getting paid, of course. We're all in it as a family. I grew up on a farm with my parents and grandparents, and my other grandparents in the neighbouring farm, so my childhood was in the countryside, and I have always grown up with all my relatives working together and making food together, slowly, taking care of the animals and growing vegetables, using what we have on the farm. I'm used to that way of living and working together as a family. We also learned what to do with the food and what to serve, and the regional traditions; it's really in my heart. That was what we wanted to create here. We call it the Vikgården *kaffebu*, it's a coffee shop that's also built on the history of what was here in Sjøgata. In the past, people from the area came to Mosjøen to buy coffee. There were a lot of small cafés in Sjøgata in those days. There is a real history in Mosjøen with all the coffee places that doesn't exist in Mo i Rana, Sandnessjøen, Brønnøysund, and the towns around us. It's a tradition in Mosjøen to go to cafés. And today, still.

That's why we call it Vikgården, and second to that it's a trade shop, *landhandel*, and a coffee place. We serve coffee and something to have with it. It has grown during the years to be a kind of restaurant, with a lot of guests. We have had [guests] from all over the world over the years, and what all they love is the "shoulders down" atmosphere, which is based on us, the family behind the tradition, and the food from the area. So we think maybe that's the reason why a lot of people have enjoyed coming here and staying with us.

At Vikgården you feel at home right away, but also when you step through the doors it feels like you've gone back in time, so you're in a dream, almost.

M: We have always thought about what makes it so special because we have felt that all the guests enjoy being here and being taken care of, and I think it is the relaxing atmosphere. Nowadays you can buy everything for money, you can travel all around the world; there's good food all over. It has to be something else. And I think that's what is here and what makes it so good. It's reliable and it's down to earth.

Yeah, it's definitely the family component that you describe: feeling your presence – you and the whole family, and your connection to this place; feeling like an extension of your family when you come through the doors.

M: Making people kind of relax. And everybody's welcome, it's not only for people with a lot of money; we have a lot of guests that I know have some troubles in life and they are not afraid to step into our place. There's room for everybody and we try as hard as we can to have a conversation with everyone who comes in.

You have an amazing collection of antiques at Vikgården. I'm curious when you started collecting, and how you found such amazing items?

M: Per Einar's always hunting for antiques. He has been collecting stuff for years. He's still hunting! Sometimes we argue, "Now it's enough." There is no room for anything else! I like everything to have its own place.

PER EINAR: I've always loved antiques. So when we started the café, I began aggressively hunting. I asked a lot of people, but I learned not to ask too much, but in a kind way, in the right way. And I have been very lucky. A lot of the stuff in Vikgården is from this area, from the streets.

M: And from Norway as well.

PE: Especially North Norway, yeah. I like that best. We also have the boat, a Viking ship, which is kind of the same; around the time Vikgården was built, they would use this kind of boat to sail to Lofoten for fishing in January, February, March. It's my job in Vikgården, and I am also the dishwasher. The best dishwasher in the world, I think.

What are some of your favourite items that you've found over the years?

PE: I like all the signs. Some of the signs I found in this house.

M: He found them under the floor!

PE: That was in the beginning. But it's very low down there, so now I'm too fat to go and find more.

M: It's too late.

PE: The original things from the house are very good to have.

And the fireplace, is that original?

M: It's not. There was a fireplace like that from the old days, so there has always been a place for it, and it was important to keep warm.

PE: We use it every day in the winter time. And I think that's also a part of the atmosphere here, because wherever you're coming from, you can warm up. So it's an important thing.

Absolutely. And the wolf cloaks? Where did they come from?

PE: We have a special arrangement in Røros two hours from Trondheim. In the winter, in February, there are maybe eighty horses that come into the market. The traders wear these coats when they are sitting on the sled, behind the horse, to keep warm in the winter. We had been there a few times and I thought these coats were very nice. So we bought two – one wolf and one dog, and we have a third as well. And this chef –

M: I think it was Paul Cunningham who found them the first time. And after that it has been a competition about who wants to be the one this year to have their picture taken in the coat.

Speaking of chefs, can you talk a little bit about some of the food that you make at Vikgården?

M: We use a lot from the local farmers, the local producers. So I can't set the menu until I find out what's possible to get from the people around us, what they have in store. I remember there were some guests that tried to say, "but you could just buy it from a supermarket," or "you could just do this and that." And I said, no, that's not the value of the place. It needed to be our way. So we work really hard with the local producers. I think that's very special here in Mosjøen, because it's a slow city. There is not very much happening every day. It's really quiet around here. And then when we arrange something, there's a huge amount of people coming into the city to enjoy it. We work together and then things happen, so we're not just waiting for others to do – we are a doer city. Everybody's working together. *Dugnad*, we say in Mosjøen. We call it *dugnad* when we work for free together and make things happen. It's like they do it in the countryside.

I wonder if you could talk a bit about the mountain farm – the history of the place and your connection to it?

M: Per Einar's family, his father's aunt, was married to the neighbouring farm in the area. There are only three farms in the area: Eldsmo, where we are, Harvasstua, and Sjånes. Only three farms up there in the mountain, and one of them is ours. Per Einar grew up going to Harvasstua. They built a cabin there when he was young. And we have been together since I was fifteen, so we started going up there together. We have spent every available moment up there from the beginning, and we were supposed to take over a place up there. That was the original dream.

The traditional wolf cloaks that hang at Vikgården were made specifically for mountain dwellers travelling by horse-drawn sledges in winter. They are thick, heavy, and long — almost like a great weighted blanket.

The tradition of waffle-making in Norway is one which dates back hundreds of years. Classic combinations include Norwegian brown cheese (*brunost*) — or simply salted butter — and jam. In North Norway, lightly macerated cloudberries may take the place of jam, as shown here.

PART 2
ELDSMO:
MOUNTAIN FARM

We have always been connected to the mountains and wanted to start a business up there. But we were waiting for ten years and we didn't get the chance to get the place in the end. The guy at Eldsmo, he was an old guy called Inge Eldsmo. He didn't have a wife or any kids, and he was really into the idea that we were supposed to move up there with our kids and the family. He was kind of a grandfather to our kids and he lived a lot of his life through us. And when we didn't get the chance to get that place, he offered us his place. But he felt kind of shy because he felt it was a really small place and didn't hold any interest for us because it was old – a lot of it was not taken good care of; it was kind of falling down. But he gave it to us. And that was also the same year that we bought Vikgården. So in 2003, everything happened!

I was working at Vikgården every day, and on the weekends as well. I remember I would drive up to the farm on Saturday when we closed the café. I would go up and Per Einar and some of the kids would be there and I would come up just for one day and then back again. It has really been a labour of love.

PE: It's very important to us.

Can you walk us through some of the farm's history?

M: There is a special history because in the area, from the beginning, there were only the Sámi people, which was a nomadic way of living. They kept their reindeer in the area in the summertime, and then they moved back to Sweden in wintertime. Around 1900, they had to start leaving their traditional way of living. So it was a Sámi guy that built Eldsmo. And at least three of the buildings were from that time: part of the barn, the old house that we are living in, and one of the small outbuildings for goats. It's a very special history that we try to take care of. And then Inge's parents moved there in 1935, so Inge's family had it for two generations before we got it.

PE: For the Sámi people it was good to be on this side of the river, because it was closer to where the reindeer were grazing. We have a bridge; it's forty metres long. So it was a good place for the Sámi people, but it was not a good place for a farmer because it's on the wrong side of the river.

M: And that's also maybe why it has never been a huge farm.

PE: No tractors –

M: Yeah, we still use old ways of working.

Do you know what the previous owners were growing or raising?

M: Most of it was using what was already in the area. Inge's mother had a certificate on the wall that she had gotten for taking very good care of what's in the area: berries and mushrooms and herbs and whatever was growing around.

They had goats and sheep with them when they moved up here, and there was no bridge, so they put them on the boat and they came over the river. There are a lot of berries in the area, so they picked a lot of them, and I know that they also tried to grow potatoes. But I think they were difficult to keep – they were lucky that in good years they could manage to get a lot of potatoes, but sadly they lost them often. I don't think they did it for very many years.

PE: When they first moved there, they couldn't afford a horse. They had an ox. After the first year, they got their first horse – one of the horses the Germans used in the war, so they got it cheap.

M: Also during those ten years, I was working on a European project which was with Norway and Sweden, and I was paid to work with culture and tourism in the area. So in that period we also learned a lot about the history in the area and the history of the Sámi people from the beginning and the Norway-Sweden collaboration. We are very fond of this place and the closeness to Sweden.

PE: This area is very connected to the Swedish people on the other side. The people in this area are very Swedish and the Swedish people in the neighbouring area in Sweden are very Norwegian, so we have a very good connection. In the old days they used horses and sledges. They came from Sweden to go to Mosjøen and pick up what they needed –

M: And to sell their own stuff.

So it was a popular trading point.

M: You can see over the border to Sweden. We also have Norway's only wild national park, which is right behind our farm. It's a really, really beautiful area around us.

The Land

Something that I remember very fondly is just how you kind of disconnect from the world, being up in the mountains, and there's very little internet or Wi-Fi and the world is what's in front of you and not what's on your phone or the chaos of a city. It's an incredibly relaxing and gratifying experience.

M: I agree with you. We have no neighbours around, so in wintertime when it's dark, it's really dark outside. You can see the stars very clearly. It's very quiet, there are no cars around; we don't have any cars on the farm, we leave them near the river. The bridge is not for driving over, so it's very quiet. You feel that you're going back in time. And our children, they're grown up now, but they still have Eldsmo in their soul. Like when they're up there, it's quietness that is important. If you want to talk to somebody on the telephone, you need to leave it in the right place, otherwise it doesn't get reception. I think that they really enjoy it, the life that they have there.

I remember it's not on any map. But I think there's something very beautiful in that, and also very connected to the work that you've done at Vikgården. There's a connection between that and the farm in terms of celebrating the heritage and a different pace of life, and an intimacy, a very personal connection to what you're doing.

M: They go really well with each other; they're built on the same history that is connected to the trade from up in the mountains down to the coast. The people that were living up there also got their stuff from Mosjøen. We keep sheep up there, and when they were slaughtered we used to bring some of the meat to Vikgården and use it in the food here. And also the berries that we picked there, we used those here, and the mushrooms. And our way of taking care of old things and old history and old tradition is very important in both places. So I think it's important in both our lives.

It's like you've created your own ecosystem.

M: Definitely. It's like the regenerative way of thinking, using what you already have. In these days when you can buy everything for money, it's difficult to get people involved and to make them say, "Wow, what a place," because there's so much money all over, it's our way of showing that you can improve what's already around you. Look in new ways, use your eyes, use your feelings, that's what people need today.

PE: That's the reason I collect old stuff.

You have a lot of old Sámi coffee cups and knives, and I was wondering if those were from the farm or from the area?

M: Yes, and some of the knives were made by Inge's brother who also grew up there. He lived on a farm ten kilometres away, in the direction of Mosjøen. And a lot of the other cups Inge made out of bark. The family of Per Einar's father that lived on the farm also made a lot of them. So they're made by the people from the area.

I wanted to ask what feelings you think of when you think of North Norway and what you want to share with the people who walk through the door?

M: It takes you back in time, kind of, but also it makes us focus on nature and tradition. It's a good place to live, up north; there's a lot of space. It's a down-to-earth way of living, but of course it's difficult for us as well because the government is making it hard to have this kind of living nowadays; it's hard for the farmers to get enough money out of the business. Fisherman as well. We are all working very hard, but industry is taking over, buying up land. It's never enough. "We need it. We need it. We need it."

And with the national park, suddenly people start to say "OK, maybe it shouldn't be a national park anymore. We need to have windmills over there." I think we are too greedy, people on Earth. But what we have been talking about now as well, and what we see about North Norway is that there's still the opportunity to slow down a bit and to live life in another way, because ninety percent of the people that are going to doctors today are sick from the lifestyle, the way of living. So maybe it's time to try to look around and see what is around us. Maybe there's another way.

To repair one of the farm's original buildings, the house was completely disassembled and rebuilt, plank by plank, by Per Einar. The traditional living roof provides an extra element of insulation.

The interior of the farmhouse is decorated with antique furniture sourced by Per Einar from nearby farms and villages. Old photos of the farm and the families that have lived there over the generations are framed and hung on the walls.

More than twenty years ago, Inge, Eldsmo's previous owner, began sharing his intimate knowledge of the forests with Marianne, showing her different routes to the cloudberries and chanterelles which have grown here for generations.

The cloudberries typically ripen in August, and store easily: when jarred, they actually self-preserve into something like a thick jam or compote, but they also freeze well. Marianne doesn't pick every mushroom or berry she finds, but she's still able to forage kilos of each to be used fresh and preserved throughout the year.

The Land

Per Einar often fishes down by the river, which is in fact the same one which runs through their hometown of Mosjøen (the Vefsna). After catching trout, he prepares them with butter and grills them, before eating them for lunch with *kamkake* — a traditional and almost cracker-like flatbread with characteristic "bubbles."

We slept just one night at Eldsmo, but I could have stayed there an eternity. That morning, after coffee and home-cooked breakfast, we walked through the frosted grass, sheep at our heels, up into the woods. Slowly, thoughtfully, we meandered up the mountain, picking berries and chanterelles, spotting where the cloudberries grew (the ones we'd eaten for dessert the night before, warmed and topped with cream). This was all knowledge Marianne had inherited from Inge, the man who'd tended to the farm and the land almost his entire life.

Now, at the top of the hill, Marianne showed us where moose hunters had recently passed through and made camp, their firepit still laid and charcoals visible.

The sun at our back, we sat down on a rocky outcrop, and stared out at the surrounding landscape – open in every direction, here and there forests cascading down mountains and through the valleys that lay in the distance. Autumn was everywhere: the hills a deep red, trees gilt in rich yellow and amber. A profound quiet swept over us, as we took in every measure of what lay before us.

We took a long and scenic detour out from Eldsmo, through the forested hills of Susendal, where we re-tread old crossroads that once served Swedish and Sámi traders travelling over the mountains. Thanks to the generosity of local farmers, we broke for coffee and food at two farms, Furuheim Gård and Sæterstad Gård, where the glow of golden hour evoked the very height of autumnal tranquillity.

Furuheim Gård sits on the banks of the Vefsna River in Hattfjelldal. The first settlers came to this area in 1827, and the farm at Furuheim was established nearly a century later in 1920. Farming (and life in general) was tough, and locals went through long periods of scarcity and hunger which eventually depopulated much of the region — with many locals moving to America.

Today, Furuheim Gård is run by Trine and Morten Bolstad, who are primarily dairy farmers. Together they care for cows from three traditional Norwegian breeds, including many Sidet Trønderfe og Nordlandsfe (STN) — a heritage North Norwegian breed which has distinctive markings said to resemble makeup.

Siri Kobberrød and Knut Kastnes have been farming at Sæterstad Gård, in Hattfjelldal, since the 1980s. Located in the forested mountains of southern Nordland, the farm is run organically, with the animals allowed to graze freely throughout the summer months.

In addition to making their own delicious goat's milk *brunost*, Siri Kobberrød and Knut Kastnes also produce a variation on a Sámi "coffee cheese," which was traditionally made with reindeer milk. The cheese would be placed at the bottom of the coffee cup, soaking up flavour, and then eaten once the contents of the mug were drunk.

The North Cape

WILLIAM BEMENT LENT
FROM *HALCYON DAYS IN NORWAY, FRANCE, AND THE DOLOMITES*
1898

I.

The wind, cold and cheerless, blowing furiously, — the sky everywhere obscured by great heavy lowering bands of leaden clouds; — in the east a break in the gloomy expanse revealing the everlasting daylight beyond; — such was the ominous outlook as we slowly worked our way out from the protected harbour of Trondheim, into the black waters of the broad fjord at ten o'clock in the evening of July 20th on our way to the North Cape! Such departure upon a trip to which clear weather can alone give the coveted sight of the Midnight Sun and the comfort of surroundings so indispensable to full enjoyment of the peculiar scenery of the Norwegian coast, would have been discouraging and depressing, had not the weather for a week past, been so fickle and contradictory. Even this last day commenced with a hopeless dress of heavily laden clouds that looked the commencement of a prolonged storm. Yet by noon the sky was blue and well-nigh cloudless, and the atmosphere warm and delightful, apparently the beginning of settled weather. But in the evening it clouded up again. The first ten or twelve hours is said to possess but little interest.

We sat for an hour in a sheltered place and watched the tempestuous sea and the wild rock-bound coast, darkened our windows to shut the daylight out at eleven p.m. — and so ended the first of the eight eventful days. With droll consideration we were informed that in the early morning we would be exposed to the swell of the sea, and happy were they who believing, remained below. But by nine a.m., we were under the protection or within the broken barrier of islands and rocks and all was serene and lovely.

...

The coast of Norway is unique, — a sort of Thousand Islands stretched along a good thousand miles or more, but with the added charm of bold and varied mountain scenery such as one scarcely expects to find outside of peerless little Switzerland. The guide-book, glibly records that "the coast is protected by a natural barrier, *fringe* of islands." It is however, a rather uneven and irregular fringe, the kind which in dress materials would be quickly relegated to needy friends or cheerfully sent to church for missionary boxes! A cruise along the rugged and varied coast impresses one, as the days go by, with the fact that Norway must have been around when mountains, rocky islands, tiny islets and endless waters were given out. From the immense variety of forms and the tumbled irregular appearance, it looks as if she must have accepted a "job lot" and has never been really able to assort or put them in order! Mountain scenery is much the same the world over, the preponderance of certain forms and outlines alone giving a local character. But along this sea-caressed, storm-swept coastline, literally every form is seen, — the great rounded mound with its long gracefully sloping sides, — the tent like contour, — the lofty Gothic pinnacles, — the lance-like Aiguilles, — the stately castellated forms and the billowy rounding range, so full of life and motion. The islands are numberless and vary in size from a few feet to miles. The skies grew fairer, the clouds more luminous, and yet all day the heavy rainfalls were somewhere visible in the distance. We knew this day would reveal none of the greater wonders of the trip, but there was so much that was novel and enchanting we were in perpetual delight. We sat by the hour in the bow of the vessel and just *looked!* Islands there were to the right of us, islands to the left, and along the horizon a tumbled mass of purple, violet, amethyst, and blue, mingled with gold, gray- and bronze-green, — the endless line of low-lying mountains in the suppressed light. At times a bold headland, oftener a ragged, tumultuous outline of low mountains, bare of trees, save a few stunted shrubs at base, but with green of moss-like turf in patches to their very summits. But oh! the glory and beauty, the mystery and impressiveness of the bold yet soft gradation of colour in those heavy, cloud-like banks, with which we were encompassed all the day long! Sometimes a foreground of dull gray rocks, and through an opening in an apparently land-locked bay, great boulders glittering and flashing in the sunlight. Again, great deep purple mountains like sentinels, and seen between them in the beyond, a low mass of sapphire blue. Once in a great while a little house would be seen. It was impossible, though, to shake off the sense of extreme solitude and loneliness, the consciousness that these great mountain piles and rocky masses lie here *always*, year after year, basking in the sunlight, enveloped in mists and wreathed in storm clouds, while the crowd of tourists just come and go.

...

Hour after hour, like shifting scenes upon a stage with kaleidoscopic change and panoramic variety, the rocky shores, islands and strange groupings of the mountains in many a little inlet passed rapidly before us. Every moment was so full! Before you can really grasp exquisite outline or glowing colour the ceaseless movement and changing positions of the vessel opens something else equally novel or breathless, the gray rocks close in, a narrow gateway discloses a vista of bold jagged heights, with soft storm wreaths, mysterious and strange, and looking backward behold! as far as eye can reach, a new paradise of island after island, mountain beyond mountain, permeated with the wondrous blue and amethystine tints. In minor fjords the waters, mirror-like, reflected the great rocks and hills, while all around us the waves were touched with white caps. How marvellous it all seemed, seen from the deck of a steamer! While a part would be all glowing with colour or sunshine, of the mountain tops here and there it could be said, "Clouds and darkness are around about them." Anon, we came into a broad, lake-like expanse of perfectly smooth waters, with enchanting distant adamantine walls dyed with blue of sapphire and purple of amethyst. Lifting the eyes in opposite direction, away off against the blue sky and banks of pearly clouds, rose most strikingly a mass of brown and russet with deep indenture like a gateway to the cloud-land beyond. It was novel and strange, because seen from such standpoint, and enchanting, because never had we seen such wealth, delicacy and exuberance of exquisite colour.

II.

When first we reached the shadow of the great rocks, we came to Henningsvær, a very important fishing station, where in the season (midwinter) from twenty to thirty thousand fishermen are engaged. The little low islands were literally peppered with low houses and rude huts. The vessel stopped for ten minutes and then through the boundless waters continued its royal way. Oh! the solemn loneliness of that stretch of waters and those countless bare and rugged peaks! It seemed as if the Alps must be afloat! How the expression of it, "How wonderful are Thy works," oppressed mind and soul that quiet, ideal Sabbath morning! The mountain forms grew more wild, spectral, and weird. At times an outline like a Titanic saw, again great mounds of colour indescribable, or some deep inlet brilliant with ultramarine blue, or some nearer mount luminous green with the turf, with lines of purple and brown of dampened rocks. Surely, the witchery of colour never had dramatic display excelling this! Everywhere islands and islets, mountain ranges and chains, and strangely enough with all these heights, no corresponding or complementing curve or valley depth, but instead, the long soul-quieting lines of water with their solemn, grave suggestiveness of the endlessness of eternity! It was Switzerland submerged, but with the life and gladness of the happy valleys replaced by the awful immensity, solitude and utter separation from human life, of the outstretched silent waters. Something perhaps is lost of the daring, breathless towering toward the heavens, felt in valley depths, by this conscious beginning upon a level. But the inseparable mystery, solemnity, grandeur and sublimity are accentuated, and one feels farther removed from the life that now is and closer to the Unseen and nearer to the blessed life beyond. We longed for clear blue sky and continuous sunshine, yet felt in all probability we were having a greater variety of colour and atmospheric effects. It was transcendently beautiful and mysterious; was like endless worship in some grand cathedral, with here and there a column in solemn shadow and often a burst of sunlight upon occasional blue and purple peaks, like the streaming of light through clerestory stained and coloured glass.

...

Constantly changing is the configuration of mountain and hill upon every side, so that the eye wearies, the nerves grow taut with all the shifting scene of beauty and the prolonged strain of unbroken delight. A most weird and spectral scene was a row of square-cut islands like the huge abutments or piers of some gigantic bridge, and then a sharp, solitary, pyramid as we passed on through the azure and the blue. Grand and impressive as it was, we felt at times we did not gain a correct impression of the height of many of the peaks, because of the frequent handicapping by the clouds. The snow nowhere lies like a mantle covering the entire summits, or in great sweeping draperies down the mountain side, as with the Alps or Sierra Nevadas, but in spots and patches here and there as in pockets. Sometimes in the great crater-like pockets, it lay in magnificent and dazzling masses and frequently ponderous glowing glaciers seemed creeping slowly down, but oftener it was a patch, a blotch of white, upon a heraldic field of blue. The cloud effects were superb, but inasmuch as we would pass that way but once, we would willingly have dispensed with some, to have had more of unobstructed vision of lofty peak and solemn height. At one time we were in a land-locked bay, like a lake, with apparently no outlet, among the tallest peaks, over which hung and broke, Staubback like, a single thread of white waters. Such combination of beauteous form, variety of outline, sensuousness of luminous colour is said to be rare, even here. Smoothly and silently we turned into the Trollfjord; as if by magic the clouds graciously lifted, the blue sky appeared, and up and up — thousands of feet almost sheer up — on one side, rose the well-nigh bare, bald, mountain heights, with great masses of brilliant fire-weed, a few scanty shrubs and then nothing but the stupendous bare, gray rock surface. This little cove or fjord was by far the grandest and most magnificent sight we had. In this tiny bay what marvellous grandeur and sublimity! A giant mountain with smooth, slanting surface of thousands of feet from summit to water's edge; — a cone and pyramid; — streams of whitened foam coming down steep acclivities, and one great solitary glacier, made the little enclosure seem like a sanctuary, so still and holy! A single white sea-gull hovered above like the Holy Spirit brooding over the calm and repose.

...

The scene grew more rugged and wild, the peaks sharper, and the glorious sun appearing, transfigured it all. Fifteen minutes later we wondered if mountains, clouds, sky and water, could do more! One great clustered mass of purple mountains, was covered with a strange luminous cloud. The light beyond seemed to break through in long, glorious slants down their sides. A mysterious and expectant air, made it seem as if Moses had again gone up into the mount. Another peerless group of sharp-pointed and jagged peaks, with great, deep pockets filled with snow, stood out grand and sublime in the clear atmosphere. Far away, beyond a chain of low islets, a range of vivid blue mountains was broken in one place by an abrupt oblong mass like a stupendous square fortress with huge towers at the corners, all flashing in the sunshine. In another direction a solid blue, sombre mass, with broken outline of strange, weird shapes, was, in some places, monolithic in form and character. There is little use in trying to portray these details, save that they give some faint idea of the rapidly dissolving kaleidoscopic effects, gone and replaced almost momentarily.

CHAPTER TWO

The Light

Helgeland, which the old Norse called *Hálogaland*, was once a fiefdom that constituted the farthest reaches of Norse-laid settlements, and was the northernmost setting referenced in the Viking-era sagas. Today, however, it refers to a smaller stretch of land, the southernmost region of North Norway, which is characterised by the contrast of narrow stretches of coastland – populated with small, valley-based towns like Mosjøen, Mo i Rana, Brønnøysund, and Sandnessjøen – as well as a vast archipelago of over six thousand islands, with diverse landscapes from coral beaches to rugged mountains.

    Sandnessjøen is the main port town from which you can access two of the larger islands, Herøy and Dønna, and many nearby islands are further linked by a network of small bridges. Here under threat of isolation, winter storms, and tempestuous seas, daily life and livelihood depend on the strength and togetherness of the community, as it always has.

The Natural Household on the Helgeland Coast

DAGRUNN GRØNBECH

Fishing and farming in combination was a common way of life along the Norwegian coast until the 1960s. This lifestyle was based on natural households with a high degree of self-sufficiency in food and clothing. Household operations were seasonal and highly weather-dependent, and work tasks were adapted to the seasons, natural conditions, and the availability of fish. The dependence on nature entailed a respect for resources. The fisherman's family lived in harmony with nature and maintained an ethical outlook on life which can be called religious in nature.[1]

A WAY OF LIFE

Being a fisher-farmer was a way of life rooted in two primary industries; if the fishing failed, one could rely on the yield from agriculture. The combination of fishing and agriculture on a small scale was based on scarcity; saving, reuse, and the recycling of materials was therefore necessary. The natural household consisted of the extended family, in which both children and the elderly had to participate, their tasks adapted to gender roles and physical ability. The work was thus inclusive and communal. Within each community, the work was organised according to traditional gender roles, with the elderly as teachers. The transfer of knowledge took place via practical exercise and was handed down from mother to daughter and from father to son, in contrast to today – now, the younger people in many cases teach the older.

The household's subsistence was based on self-sufficiency with a low economic return. The extended family's living and working community was based on self-production, and a high degree of independence. Sheep were essential livestock, and the family procured raw materials such as meat, fish, and potatoes which were stored or preserved with the aim of lasting the year. Neighbours exchanged both goods and services, while the sale of the fish was regulated by the market economy.

POSITION OF WOMEN

For women in Norway, getting married, up until the 1960s, meant being supported by their husbands. Women and men worked in parallel, with their tasks divided by gender. The way of life was not only physically demanding, but also required mental strength. Daily life was characterised by frugality, saving, and recycling. For the children, this meant that they had to eat the food that was served and dress in home-made clothes.

Herøy church is often called "the Cathedral of Helgeland."
Credit: Helgeland Museum, avd. Herøy

In the fisher-farmer's household, the woman was not only a mother, wife, daughter, and daughter-in-law, but also a homemaker. She was responsible for a variety of tasks such as cleaning, cooking, sewing clothes, barn work, and charity work. Coastal women acted as teachers, nursing assistants, social workers, nutritionists, and household economists. In addition, the coastal woman had to show care towards her extended family and the rural community. In the fisher-farmer's family, marriage was a crucial cohabitation contract. Without a stay-at-home mother and housewife, it was not possible for the father to be away fishing for long periods to obtain the necessary income for the family. When we imagine the small farm operation based on manual labour with various tasks distributed over the four seasons, we must take into account that neither electricity nor running water in the houses was common in rural Norway before the end of the 1950s, which meant that good health and physical strength were important. In these communities, working was seen as a duty, and work as a virtue was included as part of the Protestant teaching often cited as "working by the sweat of one's brow." The older women referred to the catechism that one should not accumulate material treasures on Earth; frugality was seen as a virtue.

REUSE AND RECYCLING

Securing the food supply was a woman's task and responsibility, while the father was responsible for the boat, the fishing gear, and the fishing. During the Lofoten fishing season from January to April, the husband was not at home and the wife was left with sole responsibility and the fear that he might perish at sea. The financial surplus from the winter fishing was prioritised for upgrading the boat and fishing gear. The man's work domain was thus put first.

WORK DIVERSITY AND VALUES

The coastal people were brought up with the idea that the sea both "gives and takes," as can still be read on the wall pictures of the prayer houses on the small islands.[2] The catch and the outcome at sea were often linked to uncertainty and to good or bad luck. The fact that the fisherman knew the local fishing grounds, the conditions at sea, and took account of the sea current was part of the acquired knowledge of experience. That one did not always succeed in catching was linked to superstition; to prevent accidents, one had to take care, for example, to turn the boat with the sun. On board the boat, one was not allowed to mention names that could be associated with the barn.

LEFT: Women's work tasks throughout the year

The household was based on two industries which ensured a level of security. The livestock consisted of two to three sheep, chickens, and a pig, which were acquired in the spring and slaughtered at Christmas. Those who had land for a cow field were then given milk, which was status-conferring. It was only the large farms that had horses.

BELOW: The natural household's resource utilisation and recycling in a biodynamic circle

The model shows the sheep's importance in a total exploitation chain that includes wool, lamb, and meat. The waste from the compost pile was used as fertiliser on the meadow, and as feed for the sheep.

The Natural Household on the Helgeland Coast

Women milked the cows by hand.
Credit: Helgeland Museum, avd. Herøy

Among other beliefs, the word "horse" should preferably not be mentioned and waffles should be avoided on the boat.

TO TREAT ONE'S NEIGHBOUR AS ONESELF

The Helgeland coast consists of many islands and islets that were inhabited before the Second World War. One therefore had to travel by boat to the church. There was great respect for the priest, as God's representative on Earth. Although the fisherman worked continuously from early morning to late evening, Sunday was considered a public holiday, to be respected as a day of rest, even though the women had to cook and do barn work. The well-being of the local community depended on neighbours helping and supporting each other, and children were taught "to see one's neighbour as oneself." Neighbourly support was based on reciprocity and exchange of services and can be characterised as a moral of reciprocity: "If you help me, I'll help you." Taking care of the extended family and one's neighbour characterised the way of life as part of the collective conscience. In the local community, it was dishonourable if one did not help neighbours in need. Caring for others implied a commitment to share and not accumulate too much for oneself, which legitimised a puritanical way of life. On the Norwegian coast, the Protestant ethic and doctrine of faith measured a fisherman's hard work and sobriety in scarcity. The way of life and values were characterised by the necessary sharing of resources.

After the Second World War, technological industrial investment contributed to growth in the urban centres, drawing farmers from the rural districts and leading to the decline of this way of life. When the fisherfolk were given other opportunities in the 1960s, many parents advised their children not to continue in the drudgery of work characterised by poverty and uncertainty. The post-war generation of children of the fisher-farmers were encouraged to get an education in order to obtain a more secure livelihood with a fixed salary and a less physically demanding job. Gradually, these shifts led to a changed view of the natural landscape from being a source of livelihood to a place for holidays and recreation, which remains true to this day.

REFERENCES

1. The article is based on Dr D. Grønbech's thesis: Coastal Women's Life and Work. From Natural Household to Living Alone. A Description of Dignity. The University of Tromsø, 2008. The thesis is based on interviews with elderly women on the coast of Helgeland, who have recounted their lives as fisher-farmers. The women were born around 1915.

2. In the period 1895–1904 alone, an average of 208 fishermen died in Norway each year (Åsa Elstad: Kystkvinner i Norge. 2004:90).

Driving north out of Mosjøen and along the coast, we take a detour to a village called Bardal where Åshild Blyseth, a chef and cultural researcher, runs a cáfe-cum-folk museum called Wangbrygga i Bardal.

While a trading point of some sort has stood here for four hundred years, this wooden building dates back to the 1870s and was fully restored in the early '90s.

Wangbrygga's main room and entryway, painted a cheery yellow, is laid out like a nineteenth-century general store with old medicines and household brands, glassware, and tools, as well some remarkable antique kitchenware like intricately patterned waffle irons. Upstairs, a former storehouse is divided into rooms that are outfitted as if for lodgers, with small beds and beautiful handmade patterned blankets.

Many of those who journey the distance to Bardal do so for Åshild's traditional home-cooking. They typically visit on Sundays, when Åshild prepares a beautiful and elaborate buffet spread of traditional Norwegian dishes made from local produce. Åshild is also known for her pastries, which she bakes fresh every morning – cinnamon rolls as well as a speciality that locals call *Hemnesværinger*, a soft, sugar-dusted custard buns, named in a tongue-in-cheek manner after the denizens of nearby Hemnes.

On the day of our visit, midweek, there is no lunch offering, but Åshild is kind enough to make us a "small" spread – a hearty fish soup with halibut and salmon, bread with salted butter, *flatbrød* (a traditional crispy flatbread), fresh strawberries, lingonberries, and cherries, as well as different types of small open-faced sandwiches, made with local cheeses, meats, smoked fish, and spiced fruit.

Åshild sends us off with enough food to last us until we reach the islands, including, to my delight, two of the Hemnesværinger. Perched on the pier amidst a small scattering of buildings, we enjoy the grace of some summer sun as house martins (blue-capped swallows) and oystercatchers busy themselves amongst the rocks.

Hemnesværinger are made fresh every
morning at Wangbrygga, with locals often
ordering a tray or two for special occasions.

The Light

Leaving Wangbrygga, we drove west through the small port town of Sandnessjøen, past plaques and museums memorialising legendary figures of the little-known northernmost Viking kingdom, and boarded a ferry bound for Herøy. What we knew of this small archipelago could fit onto a postcard with room to spare: it was the birthplace of the seventeenth-century poet Petter Dass – who we'd seen cast in bronze with arms outstretched in Sandnessjøen's town centre – where narrow sea-flanked roads and rocky beaches gave you the feeling you were never more than a couple feet from the water. But we also knew it to be a place which, by reputation, was in turns both stunning and unforgiving: with countless small islands and dramatic vistas of unparalleled beauty, as well as tempestuous weather, locals lost to the waves or rocks, and a landscape ill-suited for sustained wide-spread farming.

    Yet we immediately found it to be a place of considerable charm: somewhere which, we'd later reflect, seemed to call you back to it. Here we settled into the charm and comfort of our rooms at a restored schoolhouse, Skolo, and after a restful sleep and good breakfast, set out to explore the islands before us.

Marte & Eric

In the summer of 2021, an event hosted by ArktiskMat ("Arctic Food"), the Mosjøen-based North Norwegian food symposium, drew Eric and Marte Ryan five minutes down the road from their house to Skolo, a former schoolhouse-turned-multipurpose-venue space. There, they were captivated by a talk from social historian Dagrunn Grønbech on the history of the local *fiskebønder*, or fisher-farmers. The unique lifestyle of the fiskebønder, which was once prevalent in this region, emphasised living in tune with both land and sea, using the most of the natural resources around them in order to survive periods of scarcity and difficult winters when the adult men were often away fishing. The talk was both inspiring and affirming for the couple who had recently moved up north in a bid to live more independently; a fitting way of entwining both their personal and professional interests, while respecting local traditions.

Marte (née Fossland) met Eric (an American expat) on a skiing trip in the Alps when they were in their early twenties. When they eventually moved in together in Trondheim, they found themselves out on the slopes skiing or hiking almost every weekend. The Covid-19 pandemic lured them some three hundred miles north of the city to Herøy, the Helgeland islands where Marte's family roots went back five generations. In a house and farm once owned and lived in by her great-great-grandmother, Marte and Eric began to adjust to the pace of island life, spending many an early morning or late evening outdoors.

Living on the island, they found themselves out on the water more often than not, a place of comfort for both, especially Eric, who had grown up sailing with his family in Alaska. A boat allowed them to unlock the breadth and diversity of Helgeland's almost innumerable islands, from white coral beaches amidst azure waters to meadow-capped rocky outcrops inhabited by nesting seabirds.

Their heritage-inspired project, Nordvær ("Northern Weather"), launched in 2023 as the convergence of their love for outdoor adventure and their respect of the intimate and historic balance between life and livelihood found on land and sea. Eventually it became the name of their catamaran, the centrepiece of their project, on which they host guests looking to unlock the Northern landscape in all its senses. From on-the-boat halibut fishing to scallop diving, foraging, paddleboarding, and kayaking, the day's activities often dictate the evening's meals. On their farm, Marte and Eric grow potatoes, carrots, onions, rocket, beets, and also forage down by the biodiverse tidal beaches where sheep graze – often preserving or fermenting to bolster their larder through the year. Meals each day – from freshly baked sourdough made while anchored off-island, to intricately-prepared Nordic-style dinners onboard – are prepared with the same deep respect for their surroundings.

Even for this couple, so enmeshed in active exploration of the outdoors, some of the greatest moments are in quiet stillness, and the deep appreciation of the natural beauty of the landscape that comes in contrasting moments: in winter, at night, with the wind at your back and Northern Lights shining above; on a clear summer day with the water still as glass; or autumn days at home, watching dusky orange sunsets spread across the sea.

The Light

Whether out with guests or relaxing on their own time, Eric and Marte spend much of their time on the water. Some of their favourite activities include kayaking, fishing, and free diving for scallops, which can be eaten fresh from the sea or brought home and cooked.

The farmhouse Eric and Marte live in has been in Marte's maternal family, the Toftesunds, for several generations. Along with the house, they inherited family photo albums and old cookery books (including one devoted entirely to fish dishes), as well as "domestic" guides on managing a household which had been kept in the family.

Day and Night

FROM
HALF HOURS IN THE FAR NORTH:
LIFE AMID SNOW AND ICE
1878

The farther north you go in voyaging along the coast during the months of June and July the brighter and longer becomes the daylight, until at last you arrive at the regions of perpetual day.

The charm of this state of things is beyond the comprehension of those who have not experienced it. Apart altogether from the gladdening influence of sunshine, there is something delightfully reckless in the feeling that there is no necessity whatever for taking note of the flight of time — no fear lest we should, while wandering together, or perchance alone, among the mountains, be overtaken by night. During several weeks we lived in the blaze of a long nightless day.

While we were in this bright region most of us laid aside our watches as useless, leaving it, if I remember rightly, to the skipper of our yacht to tell us when Sunday came round, for we always, when practicable, spent that day at anchor, and had service on board.

I do not use hyperbolical language when speaking of this perpetual daylight. During several weeks, after we had crossed the Arctic circle, the sun descended little more than its own diameter below the horizon each night, so that it had scarcely set when it rose again, and the diminution of the light was insignificant; it did not approach in the slightest degree to twilight. If I had suddenly awakened during any of the twenty-four hours in the cabin of the yacht, or in any place from which it was impossible to observe the position of the sun, I could not have told whether it was night or day!

Having said that, it is almost superfluous to add that we could, even in the cabin, read the smallest print at midnight as easily as at noonday. Moreover, a clear midnight sun was absolutely brighter than a cloudy forenoon. Nevertheless, there was a distinct difference between night and day — a difference with which light had nothing to do.

I am inclined to think that the incalculable myriads of minute and invisible creatures with which God has filled the solitudes of this world, even more largely than its inhabited parts, exercise a much more powerful influence on our senses than we suppose.

During the day-time these teeming millions, bustling about in the activities of their tiny spheres, create an actual, though unrecognisable noise. I do not refer to gnats and flies so much as those atomic insects whose little persons are never seen, and whose individual voices are never heard, but whose collective hum is a fact that is best proved by the silence that follows its cessation.

In the evening these all retire to rest, and night is marked by a deep impressive stillness, which we are apt erroneously to suppose is altogether the result of that noisy giant man having betaken himself to his lair. Yet this difference between night and day was only noticeable when we were alone, or very quiet; the preponderating noises resulting from conversation or walking were more than sufficient to dispel the sweet influence.

We were often very far wrong in our ideas of time. Once or twice, on landing and going into a hamlet on the coast, we have been much surprised to find the deepest silence reigning everywhere, and, on peeping in at a window, to observe that the inhabitants were all in bed, while the sun was blazing high in the heavens.

Sometimes, too, on returning from a shooting or fishing expedition, I have seen a bush or a tree full of small birds, each standing on one leg, with its head thrust under its wing and its round little body puffed up to nearly twice its usual size, and have thus been reminded that the hours for rest had returned.

Ingrid & Remi

Ingrid Erøy and Remi Fagervik have made a home for themselves in a place where land and sea meet. The couple lives on the shoreline of Seløya, a small Helgeland island, in a former boat slipway that they've converted into an idyllic seaside homestead – and a perfect setting to raise their two daughters, Nora and Lotta.

While they hail originally from different ends of the country, Ingrid and Remi both grew up in small village environments where a closeness to nature was important. After over a decade living together in Oslo, with young Nora in grade school and Lotta just born, they began to pine for that openness, the proximity to nature, and the close connections of community – a place where their daughters could grow and explore freely.

Seløya is also the island where Remi's father was born and raised, and where his grandparents lived for most of their lives. Many of his childhood memories are of visiting his grandmother and the home she lived in, which still belongs to the family. Remi's paternal grandparents were active members of the local community for decades, running a Sunday school as well as the children's association, Vårsol ("spring sun"), and organising the yearly Christmas plays and performances.

In 2011, shortly before their second daughter Lotta was born, this family connection lead Ingrid and Remi to purchase an old boat slipway ("Slipen") – a dilapidated building on a wooden pier built into the sloping shoreline – just a few minutes walk from Remi's grandmother's home. The building was in total disarray, and the renovation process required them to dig up over thirty thousand kilograms of scrap metal in order to convert and extend the structure into a home where they could comfortably spend their holidays. In time they designed and built out a space clad in a warm ply, with wide open windows highlighting long, unobstructed views over the sea, and wildflowers creeping up the glass from the garden outside.

On a holiday up north in 2018, Remi ran into the owner of the old local schoolhouse – long since shuttered, but where many of the island's inhabitants including Remi's father had gone to school – and the two began speaking about the future of the building. It turned out the owner was open to buyers, and when Remi brought this news back home, he and Ingrid jumped at the opportunity to breathe new life into the old space.

Later that year, the family moved to Seløya permanently. Since then, the new generation of the Fagervik family has quickly adjusted and integrated into the local culture. Now Lotta can easily take the family dog for daily walks, and Nora often hikes up nearby mountains with friends.

This wasn't the first time that the couple had embarked on such an ambitious project while juggling their own careers. For many years the pair had run a coffee bar and shop out of the Oslo showroom which housed their colourful childrens' brand called BLAFRE, founded back in 2005. Remi oversaw the schoolhouse's extensive renovation, with work beginning in winter of 2019: a total conversion of the building into a ground-floor café with pizza kitchen and boutique shop, a private studio and workspace, and several guest rooms which they designed and outfitted themselves. The space can also host weddings, talks, and dinners, acting as a sort of local event hall. The name they chose, Skolo ("school"), is a nod to the history of the building and the former "Seløy skole."

Skolo opened its doors in the summer of 2020, and while Ingrid and Remi have continued to develop the space inside and out – including a large outdoor dining and event space – much of Remi's time is now spent in the kitchen, mixing and shaping their cold-rise pizza dough and churning out the seasonal pies that locals love. Flavour-driven curiosity is something that Remi's father, an avid cook, passed on to him at a young age, and a clear way of bringing that familial connection into his kitchen. Whenever possible, Remi is out foraging mushrooms or flowers, pickling vegetables, and making syrups, but he also uses a range of locally sourced cheeses, meats, and fish. On long summer nights, with the restaurant space abuzz and full of laughter, it's easy to understand just how much Skolo has added to the community.

During the off-season, the café is filled with locals sipping coffees in cosy nooks, or sampling a number of homemade cakes and pastries including Skolo's own "skolobolle," a riff on the traditional Norwegian *skolebrød* – an iced, coconut-topped custard bun.

In the years since Skolo opened, Ingrid and Remi have turned their attention back to their home, enhancing the space around the building in ways that allow them to find greater comfort in, and connection to, the outdoors: a sun-facing self-contained annexe for guests, a greenhouse studio for relaxing and eating home-baked pizzas, and a wood-burning sauna. Summer days might begin with an early morning swim and a coffee enjoyed while drying off; it might end by taking the boat out for midnight fishing, followed by a fried fish sandwich under bright red skies.

In summer the days are as busy as they are long, with new guests arriving at Skolo daily, frequent socialising with friends and strangers alike, and long hours in the heat of the café's kitchen where Nora has (for the last five seasons) helped Remi. Winter, by many metrics, is calmer. Birds migrate south with the tourists, leaving a stillness in the air, and on fair-weather days only the sound of the waves or wind can be heard – in the soft winter light it leaves much time for slow moments, thinking, and appreciation. The new sauna has also given way to a weekly tradition all the more special in winter, as the family heats up inside before plunging into the ice cold waters just a couple of metres beyond.

Ultimately, it is that link with the water itself – most obvious, but also most accessible – that makes all the difference. Living on the water, they cannot help but become active parts in the local ecosystem, appreciating the changes both subtle and strong, as life ebbs and flows through the years.

Skolo's warm and friendly feel is down to the family behind it. While Remi can often be found leading renovations or in the kitchen, Ingrid is hard at work behind the scenes designing and nurturing the cosy atmosphere for guests.

The family are able to spot a dazzling array of wildlife from their living room; everything from seabirds to porpoises and dolphins — they've even spotted a pilot whale.

For a couple of weeks around the Summer Solstice, the sun doesn't set over Herøy. Instead, each night around eleven-thirty the sun slowly lowers to the horizon line — but never dips beneath it. Instead, around one or two in the morning, it begins to rise again. On clear nights, it makes for a particularly dramatic stretch of time, as sunset and sunrise effectively merge into a stunning four hour light show. Many families take this opportunity to make the most of the sun, staying up later to go for walks, hikes, or even fishing.

On this evening, Remi and Lotta caught a few cod, and Remi filleted the fish on the dock before letting the seagulls enjoy the heads and tails. The fish were then brought back inside to the kitchen, where Remi whipped up an early morning sandwich with a homemade remoulade.

We were lucky enough to stay on Herøy during Sankt Hans, the Summer Solstice, which Norwegians celebrate by gathering around a bonfire with friends and family to eat and drink.

Here on the island, we congregated by the water just a few minutes down the road from Ingrid and Remi's home. Friends joined us from Mosjøen, just a couple of hours away. Eric and Marte came as well, from much closer to home, and brought food to barbecue. There was fish caught earlier that day, grilled meat, salads, cold beers, and pastries from Skolo.

As the food cooked, Nora and Lotta joined Remi's sister, Anniken, in one of the meadows growing between the rocky beach and the main island road. There they picked flowers – *Jonsokblomst* (red campion), *Smørblomst* (buttercup), *Hundkjeks* (cow parsley) – and carefully wove them together into wild wreaths of white, yellow, and purple. Crowned, we became fitting heralds of summer.

Bellies and hearts full, the sun still high in the sky, yet the time far past midnight, we strolled back down the road to lay our heads.

ABOVE: Grilled locally hunted moose.
RIGHT: Seith (pollock) ceviche.

Mørketid

JASON BALL

From the middle of November until the end of January, North Norway is covered in a blanket of darkness. The autumn days leading up to this shift act as a sort of countdown; a bit less light every night becomes the topic of conversation during coffee the next morning. This small talk is the first sign of the inevitable – nature's colour palette slowly becomes darker, shade by shade – and we know winter is coming. The trees and foliage display that familiar autumn canopy of auburn, orange, and brown, and the sky and sunsets fall in line too, displaying the most vivid shades of pink, purple, and blue – the final bursts of colour before the night sky takes over. Eventually, when the light from the sun fades away, we are left with darkness, but it is during this time the shades of the night become much more visible.

The most obvious and perhaps the most striking example of this might be the Northern Lights, which were also the most elusive for me during my first winter in Norway. As someone who is typically in bed early most nights, my opportunities to see the Northern Lights were always missed, sleepily discovered in the morning as texts from friends that came through in the middle of the night – "Go outside now! The sky is dancing!"; "Did you see the lights?!" While this phenomenon is now well understood, there have been many myths and legends that date back to the Viking era. I've read that the Vikings believed the Lights were a reflection from the Valkyries' armour as they guided warriors to Odin; or that they were the breath of soldiers that had fallen in battles before them. In old Norse, the word *norðrljós* was used to describe them, which translates to "Northern Lights," as they are most often visible in high-latitude regions. These myths may now have been supplanted by scientific fact, but that doesn't detract from the wonder of the spectacle: a splendid and unique display of lights and colours dancing through the midnight sky – their magic best viewed in person.

There are other lights, too. They don't attract tourists and are not often written about, but they provide a warmth to many towns throughout the North in a way that the summer sun cannot. Winter brings the dark polar nights and the town turns white, as snow covers the mountaintops and rests gently on the trees. Walking around, you will find heart-shaped candles in the windows of the old historic houses along the fjord, and holiday lights hanging above Sjøgata street – a dim glow that illuminates the town. Smoke clouds arise from the chimneys of every home, sending a subtle signal that, while the town streets are indeed empty, there are people gathered around a fire at the hearth of the home. Much like the Northern Lights, the full effect must be felt in person. There is a Norwegian word – *koselig* – which can hint at this feeling; it is difficult to translate into English, but it is something I have felt on many occasions, most deeply during these dark and cold polar nights.

Norwegians will often refer to this time of the year as *mørketid*, which translates to "dark time," and after the Winter Solstice – the longest night of the year – the winter season begins. For those that haven't experienced winter in the North, there seems to be plenty of curiosity and interest about how one can endure. Friends that live elsewhere often ask: "How do you deal with it?" I will admit extreme changes in weather require adaptation – physically and mentally – but more importantly, they require acceptance. There have been many studies to suggest that changes in light and seasonality can affect one's mood and disposition – positively in some cases, and negatively in other cases – however Leibowitz & Vittersø[1] report that many of the studies that discuss the theoretical relationship between Seasonal Affective Disorder and latitude fail to take into account the adaptive ways residents in the High North, and elsewhere, shift their behaviour as the seasons change. Somehow, the residents of the High North must find a way to accept and work with the extreme winter, rather than against it.

Our first Christmas in Norway, my wife and I were visited by the *Sjøgata nisse* – which loosely translates to Sjøgata Santa. Sjøgata is the street we live on, and *nisse* is a Norwegian word that describes a character from Norwegian folklore who wore a red cap and had a long beard. He had brought a gift for us: a vacuum-packed, frozen side of wild salmon. Not only was this the first time that I was visited in my home by an adult dressed as Santa, but also the first time I had received a side of salmon as a Christmas present. At the time I thought of it as a last-minute gift, the thing you find lying around your house when you've forgotten to shop for someone – which would have been reasonable, given that we had only moved to Norway the week prior. It wasn't that at all though; as it turns out, the *Sjøgata nisse* likes to go fishing, and this gift – surprising and delicious – was from the cold and icy waters up north. It was a kind gesture that made it clear to us that we were in North Norway.

The holiday season is a delightful time to be in a small town, even if it is dark and cold. The lights, gentle snowfall, crackling fires, and visits from the *Sjogata nisse* provide a familiar feeling. When the Christmas lights come down, however, there is a sense of anticipation for what is coming; the snowfall becomes less gentle, and the darkness takes over. It's quiet, still, and cold. It feels inappropriate to be outside – almost disruptive – so instead, we take refuge and learn to experience the indoors differently. What a privilege it is when winter removes the burden of outdoor activities and social obligations; I am able to revisit my relationship to tasks or hobbies that somehow seem burdensome when the weather is "nice." Suddenly there is time to read that stack of books, prepare a more complex dinner recipe, learn a new language, or start an art project.

I find it so comforting to be stuck indoors, especially when everyone else is staying in, too. Of course preparation is important: freezers throughout the North are stocked full of fish and lamb from previous seasons; jars of jam and ferments bubble away in the pantry; the cellar is stocked with wine, and there's waffle mix in the cupboard. People in the North spend the months prior to winter preparing for it in ways that are practical – collecting wood and storing food – but they are preparing mentally, too. Just like the freezers and the pantries, the community stocks up on optimism and kindness – we don't fight the long winter, we accept it and carry on.

I've come to realise that life moves in a rhythm with the seasons in North Norway – in a way that feels required; less of a suggestion, and instead a quiet demand from nature. I didn't quite grasp this when I first moved to North Norway because I hadn't lived anywhere that was so affected by, or affectionate toward, seasonal changes. I have heard Norwegians joke that there are two seasons in North Norway: Green Winter and White Winter. A simple (and very Norwegian) explanation to describe a relatively abrupt change in scenery. After the dark winter, springtime brings a very visible awakening – suddenly everything is green. Then summer brings the Midnight Sun, which can be surprising and stunning – but for me, also highly disruptive to sleep. The trees and fields and farms are lush, the green from spring is only greener – every part of nature is thriving. The cadence of the seasons moves quietly at its own pace, while those that live in the North move along with it.

This rhythm is quite visible in nature, but it can also be found in many of the nuances of daily life. I now notice the ways in which people work with the seasons in the North. During *skrei* (cod) season, you might receive a gift of fish or roe; in springtime, a dried leg of lamb; in the autumn, smoked and dried reindeer heart; wild berries in the summer; or after a successful moose hunt – moose burgers for dinner. Just as I eventually realised during our first Christmas in Norway, these are thoughtful gifts; subtle reminders from each season that help us to acknowledge and appreciate time and place. Even during winter, when this rhythm seems to come to a standstill and the concept of time and place seems frozen (like everything else), the darkness reminds us that we must shift our attention. When nature doesn't provide these gifts, we have to seek them out elsewhere.

REFERENCES

1. Leibowitz, K., & Vittersø, J. (2020). Winter is coming: Wintertime mindset and wellbeing in Norway. International Journal of Wellbeing, 10(4), 35-54. https://doi.org/10.5502/ijw.v10i4.935

CHAPTER THREE

The Living

A small propeller plane the size of a school bus (a classy one, which distributes small squares of airline-branded chocolate) brought us within sight of Lofoten for the first time. There, with the deep red sun already half-set on the horizon, we had our first glimpse of mountains which seemed to rise from the sea. It seemed too fantastical to be real, as if it had been drawn from ancient myth or epic sagas. And yet we knew the reality to be altogether different – a place built on hard labour, salty sea air, and keen sailors.

For more than a thousand years, winter has ushered in with it a new cycle, in one of the North's greatest sagas: *lofotfiske* (Lofoten fishing). In today's society, the notional importance of fishing seasons may seem quaint, but it cannot be overstated that the economic and material survival of the North's coastline villages was dependent on the seasonal catch. Even the very makeup of these villages would change with the seasons, as thousands of fishermen left their homes for weeks or months at a time.

It is fitting then, that lofotfiske played out with intense drama: under dark skies, against biting winds, thousands of fishing boats would make their way up north along some of Norway's most remote archipelagos, where *skrei* (a migrating species of cod) had come to spawn. Here, many would risk their life to find their livelihood.

Once caught and landed, the skrei were washed and gutted, and then left to hang on wooden racks called *hjell,* where they would be dried naturally by the sun and cold winds alone. In winter, whole villages would be lined with rack after rack of hjell, with thousands of stockfish (the dried skrei) divvied up among locals and much more sent for export.

While lofotfiske does not hold the same stake for the fishing villages of Lofoten anymore, it is still a proud tradition held by these communities, where hjell still stand, a reminder of how life could be sustained for so long, and in such harsh environs, by the "simple" bounty of dried fish.

The meeting of past and present is especially visible in Henningsvær, a small village where the demands of lofotfiske once attracted hundreds of vessels at a time, creating something of a floating town in the harbour, with ships so closely packed that it's said you could walk from one side to the other without getting wet.

In the post-war days, the village bustled with activity: a dozen cod-processing factories, nearly seventy fishing facilities, dozens of stores, a handful of bakeries, mechanics, butchers, a watchmaker, and even a hat store.

In the last few decades, the construction of bridges and a surge and shift in economic activity and opportunity elsewhere in the country has changed the makeup of the village, and brought new risks to its survival. Now, a new nexus of Henningsvær has developed in an unlikely source – one of the village's former factories, Trevarefabrikken – where the linkage between generations is especially powerful, and where locals seize on the opportunity to both honour and evolve.

Henningsvær comprises two islands,
Heimøya and Hellandsøya, which are connected
by a breakwater built in the 1930s. The bridge
between the islands and the mainland was not
constructed until the 1980s, up until which time
it depended on ferries.

The season for hanging *skrei* begins around March and ends by June, when the weather begins to warm up, when the fish are collected and sold as *tørrfisk* (stockfish). The stockfish trade dates back centuries, and is one of Norway's oldest commercial exports.

The Fisherman and the Draug

JONAS LIE
FROM *WEIRD TALES FROM NORTHERN SEAS*
TRANSLATED BY R. NISBET BAIN
1893

On Kvalholm, down in Helgeland,[1] dwelt a poor fisherman, Elias by name, with his wife Karen, who had been in service at the parson's over at Alstad. They had built them a hut here, and he used to go out fishing by the day about the Lofotens.

There could be very little doubt that the lonely Kvalholm was haunted. Whenever her husband was away, Karen heard all manner of uncanny shrieks and noises, which could mean no good. One day, when she was up on the hillside, mowing grass to serve as winter fodder for their couple of sheep, she heard, quite plainly, a chattering on the strand beneath the hill, but look over she durst not.

They had a child every year, but that was no burden, for they were both thrifty, hard-working folks. When seven years had gone by, there were six children in the house; but that same autumn Elias had scraped together so much that he thought he might now venture to buy a Sexæring,[2] and henceforward go fishing in his own boat.

One day, as he was walking along with a Kvejtepig[3] in his hand, and thinking the matter over, he unexpectedly came upon a monstrous seal, which lay sunning itself right behind a rock on the strand, and was as much surprised to see the man as the man was to see the seal. But Elias was not slack; from the top of the rock on which he stood, he hurled the long heavy Kvejtepig right into the monster's back, just below the neck.

The seal immediately rose up on its tail right into the air as high as a boat's mast, and looked so evilly and viciously at him with its bloodshot eyes, at the same time showing its grinning teeth, that Elias thought he should have died on the spot for sheer fright. Then it plunged into the sea, and lashed the water into bloody foam behind it. Elias didn't stop to see more, but that same evening there drifted into the boat place on Kvalcreek, on which his house stood, a Kvejtepole, with the hooked iron head snapped off.

Elias thought no more about it, but in the course of the autumn he bought his Sexæring, for which he had been building a little boat-shed the whole summer.

One night as he lay awake, thinking of his new Sexæring, it occurred to him that his boat would balance better, perhaps, if he stuck an extra log of wood on each side of it. He was so absurdly fond of the boat that it was a mere pastime for him to light a lantern and go down to have a look at it.

Now as he stood looking at it there by the light of the lantern, he suddenly caught a glimpse in the corner opposite, on a coil of nets, of a face which exactly resembled the seal's. For an instant it grinned savagely at him and the light, its mouth all the time growing larger and larger; and then a big man whisked out of the door, not so quickly, however, but that Elias could catch a glimpse, by the light of the lantern, of a long iron hooked spike sticking out of his back. And now he began to put one and two together. Still he was less anxious about his life than about his boat; so sat down in it with the lantern, and kept watch. When his wife came in the morning, she found him sleeping there, with the burnt-out lantern by his side.

One morning in January, while he was out fishing in his boat with two other men, he heard, in the dark, a voice from a skerry at the very entrance of the creek. It laughed scornfully, and said, "When it comes to a Femböring,[4] Elias, look to thyself!"

But there was many a long year yet before it did come to that; but one autumn, when his son Bernt was sixteen, Elias knew he could manage it, so he took his whole family with him in his boat to Ranen,⁵ to exchange his Sexæring for a Femböring. The only person left at home was a little Finn girl, whom they had taken into service some few years before, and who had only lately been confirmed.

Now there was a boat, a little Femböring, for four men and a boy, that Elias just then had his eye upon—a boat which the best boat-builder in the place had finished and tarred over that very autumn. Elias had a very good notion of what a boat should be, and it seemed to him that he had never seen a Femböring so well built below the water-line. Above the water-line, indeed, it looked only middling, so that, to one of less experience than himself, the boat would have seemed rather a heavy goer than otherwise, and anything but a smart craft.

Now the boat-master knew all this just as well as Elias. He said he thought it would be the swiftest sailer in Ranen, but that Elias should have it cheap, all the same, if only he would promise one thing, and that was, to make no alteration whatever in the boat, nay, not so much as adding a fresh coat of tar. Only when Elias had expressly given his word upon it did he get the boat.

Elias now thought about sailing home, but went first into the town, provided himself and family with provisions against Christmas, and indulged in a little nip of brandy besides. Glad as he was over the day's bargain, he, and his wife too, took an extra drop in their e'en, and their son Bernt had a taste of it too.

After that they sailed off homewards in their new boat. There was no other ballast in the boat but himself, his old woman, the children, and the Christmas provisions. His son Bernt sat by the main-sheet; his wife, helped by her next eldest son, held the sail-ropes; Elias himself sat at the rudder, while the two younger brothers of twelve and fourteen were to take it in turns to bail out.

They had eight miles of sea to sail over, and when they got into the open, it was plain that the boat would be tested pretty stiffly on its first voyage. A gale was gradually blowing up, and crests of foam began to break upon the heavy sea.

And now Elias saw what sort of a boat he really had. She skipped over the waves like a sea-mew; not so much as a splash came into the boat, and he therefore calculated that he would have no need to take in

all his clews⁶ against the wind, which an ordinary Femböring would have been forced to do in such weather.

Out on the sea, not very far away from him, he saw another Femböring, with a full crew, and four clews in the sail, just like his own. It lay on the same course, and he thought it rather odd that he had not noticed it before. It made as if it would race him, and when Elias perceived that, he could not for the life of him help letting out a clew again.

And now he went racing along like a dart, past capes and islands and rocks, till it seemed to Elias as if he had never had such a splendid sail before. Now, too, the boat showed itself what it really was, the best boat in Ranen.

The weather, meantime, had become worse, and they had already got a couple of dangerous seas right upon them. They broke in over the main-sheet in the forepart of the boat where Bernt sat, and sailed out again to leeward near the stern.

Since the gloom had deepened, the other boat had kept almost alongside, and they were now so close together that they could easily have pitched the baling-can from one to the other.

So they raced on, side by side, in constantly stiffer seas, till night-fall, and beyond it.

The sea-fire, which played on the dark billows near Elias's own boat, shone with an odd vividness in the foam round the other boat, just as if a fire-shovel was ploughing up and turning over the water. In the bright phosphorescence he could plainly make out the rope-ends on board her. He could also see distinctly the folks on board, with their sou'westers on their heads; but as their larboard side lay nearest, of course they all had their backs towards him, and were well-nigh hidden by the high heeling hull.

Suddenly a tremendous roller burst upon them. Elias had long caught a glimpse of its white crest through the darkness, right over the prow where Bernt sat. It filled the whole boat for a moment, the planks shook and trembled beneath the weight of it, and then, as the boat, which had lain half on her beam-ends, righted herself and sped on again, it streamed off behind to leeward.

While it was still upon him, he fancied he heard a hideous yell from the other boat; but when it was over, his wife, who sat by the shrouds, said, with a voice which pierced his very soul: "Good God, Elias! The sea has carried off Martha and Nils!"—their two youngest children, the first nine, the second seven years old, who had been sitting in the hold near Bernt. Elias merely answered: "Don't let go the lines, Karen, or you'll lose yet more!"

The companion boat, which had disappeared in the meantime, now suddenly ducked up alongside again, with precisely the same amount of sail as Elias's boat; but he now began to feel that he didn't quite like the look of the crew on board there. The two who stood and held in the yards (he caught a glimpse of their pale faces beneath their sou'westers) seemed to him, by the odd light of the shining foam, more like corpses than men, nor did they speak a single word.

A little way off to larboard he again caught sight of the high white back of a fresh roller coming through the dark, and he got ready betimes to receive it. The boat was laid to with its prow turned aslant towards the on-rushing wave, while the sail was made as large as possible, so as to get up speed enough to cleave the heavy sea and sail out of it again. In rushed the roller with a roar like a foss; again, for an instant, they lay on their beam ends; but, when it was over, the wife no longer sat by the sail ropes, nor did Anthony stand there any longer holding the yards—they had both gone overboard.

A moment afterwards the comrade boat ducked up again: it had vanished for an instant as before. Now, too, he saw more of the heavy man who sat in the stern there in the same place as himself. Out of his back, just below his sou'wester (as he turned round it showed quite plainly), projected an iron spike six inches long, which Elias had no difficulty in recognising again. And now, as he calmly thought it all over, he was quite clear about two things: one was that it was the Draug[7] itself which was steering its half-boat close beside him, and leading him to destruction; the other was that it was written in heaven that he was to sail his last course that night. For he who sees the Draug on the sea is a doomed man. He said nothing to the others, lest they should lose heart, but in secret he commended his soul to God.

At three or four o'clock in the morning they saw coming upon them through the darkness a breaker of such a height that at first Elias thought they must be quite close ashore near the surf swell. Nevertheless, he soon recognised it for what it really was—a huge billow. Then it seemed to him as if there was a laugh over in the other boat, and something said, "There goes thy boat, Elias!" He, foreseeing the calamity, now cried aloud: "In Jesus' Name!" and then bade his sons hold on with all their might to the withy-bands by the rowlocks when the boat went under, and not let go till it was above the water again. He made the elder of them go forward to Bernt; and himself held the youngest close by his side, stroked him once or twice furtively down the cheeks, and made sure that he had a good grip. The boat, literally buried beneath the foaming roller, was lifted gradually up by the bows and then went under. When it rose again out of the water, with the keel in the air, Elias, Bernt, and the twelve-year-old Martin lay alongside, holding on by the withy-bands; but the third of the brothers was gone.

There they sat through the long dark winter night, clinging convulsively on by their hands and knees to the boat's bottom, which was drenched by the billows again and again.

After the lapse of a couple of hours died Martin, whom his father had held up the whole time as far as he was able, of sheer exhaustion, and glided down into the sea. They had tried to cry for help several times, but gave it up at last as a bad job.

Whilst they two thus sat all alone on the bottom of the boat, Elias said to Bernt he must now needs believe that he too was about to be "along o' mother!"[8] but that he had a strong hope that Bernt, at any rate, would be saved, if he only held out like a man. Then he told him all about the Draug, whom he had struck below the neck with the Kvejtepig, and how it had now revenged itself upon him, and certainly would not forbear till it was "quits with him."

It was towards nine o'clock in the morning when the grey dawn began to appear. Then Elias gave to Bernt, who sat alongside him, his silver watch with the brass chain, which he had snapped in two in order to drag it from beneath his closely buttoned jacket. He held on for a little time longer, but, as it got lighter, Bernt saw that his father's face was deadly pale, his hair too had parted here and there, as often happens when death is at hand, and his skin was chafed off his hands from holding on to the keel. The son understood now that his father was nearly at the last gasp, and tried, so far as the pitching and tossing would allow it, to hold him up; but when Elias marked it, he said, "Nay, look to thyself, Bernt, and hold on fast. I go to mother—in Jesus' Name!" and with that he cast himself down headlong from the top of the boat.

Every one who has sat on the keel of a boat long enough knows that when the sea has got its own it grows much calmer, though not immediately. Bernt now found it easier to hold on, and still more of hope came to him with the brightening day. The storm abated, and, when it got quite light, it seemed to him that he knew where he was, and that it was outside his own homestead, Kvalholm, that he lay driving.

He now began again to cry for help, but his chief hope was in a current which he knew bore landwards at a place where a headland broke in upon the surge, and there the water was calmer. And he did, in fact, drive closer and closer in, and came at last so near to one of the rocks that the mast, which was floating by the side of the boat all the time, surged up and down in the swell against the sloping cliff. Stiff as he now was in all his limbs from sitting and holding on, he nevertheless succeeded, after a great effort, in clambering up the cliff, where he hauled the mast ashore, and made the Femböring fast.

The Finn girl, who was alone in the house, had been thinking, for the last two hours, that she had heard cries for help from time to time, and as they kept on she mounted the hill to see what it was. There she saw Bernt up on the cliff, and the overturned Femböring bobbing up and down against it. She immediately dashed down to the boat-place, got out the old rowing-boat, and rowed along the shore and round the island right out to him.

Bernt lay sick under her care the whole winter through, and didn't go a fishing all that year. Ever after this, too, it seemed to folks as if the lad were a little bit daft.

On the open sea he never would go again, for he had got the sea-scare. He wedded the Finn girl, and moved over to Malang, where he got him a clearing in the forest, and he lives there now, and is doing well, they say.

REFERENCES

1. A district in North Norway.
2. A boat with three oars on each side.
3. A long pole, with a hooked iron spike at the end of it, for spearing Kvejte or halibut with.
4. A large boat with five oars on each side, used for winter fishing in North Norway.
5. The chief port in those parts.
6. The Klör, or clews, were rings in the corner of the sail to fasten it down by in a strong wind. Setja ei Klo = "take in the sail a clew." Setja tvo, or tri Klör = "take it in two or three clews," i.e., diminish it still further as the wind grew stronger.
7. A demon peculiar to the North Norwegian coast. It rides the seas in a half-boat. Comparable to the Icelandic draugr.
8. Være med hu, Mor. Hu is the Danish Hun.

Håvard Ånensen is a local fisherman with roots in Henningsvær that stretch back seven generations. After working in fisheries, he worked as a fisherman on boats across the Barents Sea, even catching king crab in Finnmark. These days he no longer fishes commercially, but instead leads fishing trips and whale-watching trips from a beautiful wooden boat called the Ørnin, which was built in 1948.

The more commercial side of the local fishing industry these days is handled in large facilities along the water, where the fish are unloaded and processed. In days long past, local boys or young men would make a little extra pocket money by cutting the tongues from the cod heads and selling them on as a delicacy, which would be sautéed in butter or battered and fried. Today, the cod cheeks are also treated with the same reverence.

The Living

Equally as breathtaking as the coast, Lofoten's mountains draw an array of visitors, from trekkers to skiiers, to their snow-capped peaks.

Trevarefabrikken

PART 1
HISTORY

Trevarefabrikken ("The wood-working factory") is a three-story, eighteen hundred square metre concrete building on the edge of the island of Heimøya in Henningsvær. The building, one of the island's biggest, was constructed in the 1940s by Alf Reidar Johansen, a second-generation Værret and entrepreneur who served on the local county board, and whose career was focused on building opportunities within the island community.

In this period, decades before the discovery of North Sea oil and bridges to the mainland, island villages like Henningsvær functioned as self-sufficient societies, places where everyone would wear a few different hats.

Trevarefabrikken embodied this reality in its early years: a woodworking factory during the warmer months, it would pivot operation during *skrei* season, when its carpenters would down their tools and move upstairs to start steaming cod liver oil, can cod roe, and even peel shrimp. In time, however, demand would necessitate that woodworking continue throughout the year, and at its height, there were around thirty carpenters, upholsterers, and painters working across the building.

Alf Reidar was eventually joined (and later succeeded) by his son Alf Per, who had grown up around the factory, and who inherited his father's zeal for work and eye for opportunity. Both father and son also benefited from the service (and friendship) of Alf Martinsen, the factory's long-time foreman, a skilled carpenter who kept a perfect attendance in his fifty-plus years of work.

By the early 2000s, as Alf Martinsen and Alf Per approached retirement, it was clear that there was neither the labour nor the demand to continue work under a new generation. Instead, when Alf Martinsen retired in 2007, full-time production ceased and only side-projects and occasional work was carried out here. In 2012, the factory was closed, and Alf Per began looking for a new owner to breathe life into the building he'd known his whole life.

LEFT: Alf Per Johansen remembers Trevarefabrikken in its earliest days — he was just a boy when his father began constructing it. He would later take over the factory from his father, and operate it until 2012 — later selling the building on to the new generation. He still lives half a block from Trevarefabrikken.

RIGHT: Alf Martinsen, Trevarefabrikken's legendary foreman, worked at the factory for decades without taking a single sick day. He specialised in building staircases, and at one point could rightly claim to have built every single one in Henningsvær. An avid hunter, during game season, he would often spend his weekends up in the mountains hunting grouse — and only gave it up in his mid-eighties.

The Living

Alf Per's father, Alf Reidar Johansen (back, far left) and Alf Martinsen (front, centre) at Trevarefabrikken in the days when it was still an operational factory.

Trevarefabrikken

**PART 2
TODAY**

Martin Hjelle and Mats Alfsen are Trevarefabrikken's new torchbearers. In 2014, they, along with their brothers (both named Andreas), childhood friends and Bergen natives, ended a two-week-long camping trip in Lofoten with a blissful final evening spent in Henningsvær. After summiting one of the local mountains, they sat together joking about how they could just stay forever, when one of their new friends mentioned that, in fact, an old factory was for sale and that they should check it out. The brothers, high on the experience of the last couple of weeks, jumped at the chance.

Before their flight left the next day, Alf Per Johansen met them at the factory for a tour of the space – sharing with them the ins and outs of the factory that his father had built, and that the two of them had managed for the last seventy years. Without a proper plan in place, the two sets of brothers pooled their savings and placed a deposit together.

For the first couple of summers, they used the factory predominantly as a sort of base camp for themselves and friends to explore Lofoten, until in late 2016 they decided to all quit their jobs and move north full-time in order to make a proper go of it.

The new chapter of Trevarefabrikken began in summer of 2017, when the brothers opened the doors of the ground floor's new café, bar, and restaurant. Over the next few years, the scope and ambition of their project broadened as they designed and built out new bespoke suites, guest rooms and a yoga studio upstairs, a wine bar and a proper pizza oven, and a sea-facing sauna. In a handful of years, the former factory has become a welcome home for those exploring Lofoten and Henningsvær, a place to stay for a week or longer and truly get to know the area. For many Norwegians and expats alike, the factory is also a draw for those hoping to emulate the brothers and their permanent move to the North – at least twenty have since followed their path. For a village of (now) five hundred and seventeen, this is not insignificant, and has effects on the wider community: for instance, three out of four teachers at the local school are former Trevare employees or part-time employees.

But despite all the newcomers, there are still the locals who make Trevare part of their daily or weekly routine. One of them is Alf Per Johansen, who still lives around the corner and visits every single day for his morning coffee. Alf Martinsen, the former foreman, is several years older and a little less mobile, although equally supportive of the new owners. The somewhat unlikely bond and friendship between these men – in particular between Martin, Mats, Alf Per, and Alf Martinsen – serves as a beautiful linkage between generations, and a natural way of honouring the past while moving forward.

A number of the architectural features of the factory were kept in its renovation. Designed by Tuckey Design Studio, these features have been folded into the fabric of Trevare — many of the original machines can still be seen in the corridors, and in some rooms the beds are tucked into the cosy alcoves of the old elevator shaft.

Ben Mervis with Martin Hjelle

Your first visit to Henningsvær was ten years ago now, right? What was the mood and the energy like for the four of you and how was Henningsvær different from the other places that you had been?

MARTIN HJELLE: It was the end of a really memorable summer vacation, and we just had our last night at the top of Festvågtind (a local mountain with a great view overlooking the ocean, Henningsvær, and Lofoten), which was quite magical. We were with a local musician from Henningsvær, Sondre Justad, who now is a big Norwegian pop star, but back then he was still emerging. We knew that we were going home, back to our studies and work and we knew the vacation was over, but we were excited because Sondre told us about this old industrial building in Henningsvær that was for sale.

The day we were supposed to leave, the previous owner of Trevarefabrikken, Alf Per Johansen, showed us around the old factory. Back then, Alf Per was seventy-four, turning seventy-five, and just a really warm, open, welcoming guy. I think he was really happy and humbled that suddenly these young guys from Bergen were taking interest in this old building, that maybe it would survive if we bought it. He was so enthusiastic, showing us around and really giving us a peek into the past and how hard the old life used to be, and that was very touching, but also extremely fascinating. He remembers names, years, dates, locations, on such a detailed level – he's a living lexicon of Henningsvær.

I remember the whole history being very overwhelming and fascinating and inspiring. At the end, we were standing in the cod liver oil room on the third floor with the view – the room that is the yoga room now – and I remember my brother saying something like, "We cannot not buy this." We didn't know what we were going to do with it, but we couldn't not buy it.

Henningsvær itself – I'm not going to say it was sleepy, it wasn't – around the time we came, it was definitely starting to become more popular among young crowds, especially young Norwegian crowds. It was one of the busier villages in Lofoten, because it still had its fishing heritage and it's picturesque, but it wasn't what it is today. I think every era has its thing, and now I feel Henningsvær is, for the time being, saved from becoming a village where only elderly people live; that is not going to happen for the next ten, twenty years, because now there is a generation shift.

Do you go to Alf Per for support or stories, for instance if you're trying to understand the building?

M: Not so much in terms of the building itself anymore, but often when it comes to Henningsvær, and relations, and people, and if things need to be fixed. We renovated the building ourselves, but we're not construction workers by trade. The other day, one of our toilets suddenly started leaking. The first person we call is Alf Per, because he has everything, but he didn't have the right size O-ring we needed. He tells us, "Call Jann at Joker (the local grocery store). Do you have his number? Actually, never mind, let's go over there together." That's typical with Alf Per. That still happens on a weekly basis. When we celebrated Pride last week, we finally managed to get some new flagpoles, but of course they needed to be painted. So at the beginning of that week, Alf Per carried flag poles around town and to his garden to paint them.

A flagpole is not a light thing, and Alf Per is what, eighty-five?

M: Yeah. Turning eighty-five in September. But he's a strong man. He drinks three litres of milk a day. A few years ago, his doctor asked him about his diet, because his cholesterol was a little high. He tells the doctor that he eats a typical Norwegian diet: sandwiches with butter and cheese, fish and potatoes, *skrei* and roe and liver and all that stuff. "And also I drink three litres of whole-fat milk every day." The doctor told him to switch to semi-skimmed and he'd be fine.

He's very involved in the community. We have this big garden in Henningsvær called Storhagen, and taking care of it has always been Alf Per's pride. Every spring he makes sure the fences are put up because they're taken down in the winter so we can snow plough. He's in charge of so much maintenance around Henningsvær that not everybody sees. A few days ago I passed the park at eight in the morning, and there was Alf Per mowing the lawn. That's a very typical sight, him just fixing things on behalf of all of us.

He's kind of like a bonus grandfather.

M: Yes. He's the bonus grandfather for a lot of the younger generation and all the people surrounding Trevarefabrikken, because he's here every day and everybody knows him.

He's a daily presence at Trevarefabrikken, right?

M: Yes; drinking coffee, inviting us over for barbecue. He actually called me last week and he was like, "I finally fired up the grill!" He was going to grill the first whale steaks of the summer, and he called and was like, "Do you want to come over?" I hadn't dared to tell him that I'm not the biggest fan of whale, but I was also really busy. So I kind of tried to mix the two and I said, "Oh, I would love to, but honestly I have a lot to do, and actually I'm not the biggest fan of whale steak." When I met him a few days later at the factory, we were just sitting having our daily coffee, and he suddenly said, "Did you know Martin doesn't actually like whale steak? What is wrong with him?"

Alf Per also introduced you to Alf Martinsen, right? Can you tell me about that relationship? They've been friends and colleagues for decades, and Alf Martinsen also worked for Alf Per's father, Alf Reidar. So they've known each other a long time, but they're quite different in a lot of ways.

M: Definitely. They have a special relationship because they've been working together for many years, and also when Alf Per took over [from his father], Alf Martinsen had been managing the carpentry workshop for so many years; he knew everything. Alf Per is a bit more old school, more of the quiet type.

Alf Martinsen came up working under Alf Per's father, and then started working for Alf Per. In some ways, he's a typical industrial, workwear man, in a very positive way. He can just do stuff. His hands are huge. I have regular-sized hands, and I think I can fit one and a half of my hands in his – they're just massive. He's not a huge guy, but he's strong. He's turning ninety-two soon. Fifteen years ago, you could drop him in the woods and he would be fine. He's a more rugged character, but he's still very authentic and honest.

Very salt-of-the-earth.

M: Very. Until last year, Alf Martinsen still went by himself to collect seagull eggs. I don't know if you know too much about seagull eggs, but they're quite huge, like three times the size of a regular chicken egg, and you shouldn't have more than two in a year because there're so many heavy metals in them. We went to his house in April or May, and when we get there, there's beer on the table, there's homemade cherry liqueur and this plum wine he makes on the table, and there's seagull eggs, salt, pepper… and nothing else. Of course I extended my limit, I ate three seagull eggs, which was lovely. I thought, okay, those were my seagull eggs for the season. A few weeks later, I met Alf Per and Alf Martinsen and I'm like, "Hey, what are you guys up to?" And they're like, "Oh, we just had another three seagull eggs." I guess they're so old, it doesn't matter anymore.

Alf Martinsen kind of taught Alf Per, in some ways.

M: Yes, I think so. I think Alf Martinsen has a huge admiration and respect for Alf Per, as he had such love and respect for Alf's father, and that has just passed on through the generations. There is this special love in a way that maybe isn't so expressive as it is between people nowadays, but still very much founded on mutual respect.

When you live in such a small community, I think the link between generations, even over time, is so clear. I was thinking about how Alf Reidar was actually born in the house that Mats lives in today. Of course that was over a hundred years ago now, but when you live in such proximity, everyone's aware of the history – you're living with the ancestors at all times, in a way. It makes heritage more important.

M: Definitely, because everything is connected, because everybody knows about everything: you live there, I live here. "Oh, you know him?"; "He was this and that for me." Interacting with the past every day in the present and preserving it for the future.

The distance from past to present in time is the same as in any other place, but I think because of proximity, and also because everybody knows each other, it makes the relationship to that distance, time and the past, feel closer because you can go and speak to people who lived in a totally different way than in Oslo or any other big city, for instance. I was at my sister's in Oslo for a wedding this weekend and when I left her apartment this morning, I really felt alienated because I don't really know any people, I don't know the connections, the history of things.

You're originally from much further south, in Bergen, which has its own special connection with Lofoten – that's where fishermen would go, and it was a major place for them to sell their wares. I'm curious if you see other links between the two places?

M: Personally, definitely. Bergen has always been a very international, continental city in some ways, if you go back historically, because of the trading connections. And where did the traders get their raw produce? Lofoten. That's what they capitalised on for all those hundreds of years: stockfish, that was the big thing. There's been a connection between Lofoten, Bergen and Europe – Denmark, Germany, the Netherlands, England, Italy, Spain – a flow of people, money, traditions, and culture going back and forth for hundreds of years. I heard a saying not so long ago that people from Bergen are just lazy Lofoten fishermen because they rowed down to Bergen with their fish in their boats and then some just stayed.

Was your vision with Trevarefabrikken to honour that past?

M: For us, what became clear in Henningsvær was this community feeling. That's what we felt when we got here, we were very quickly integrated into the existing community, and it became a directional star for Trevarefabrikken to give that feeling to people that they are a part of something. Whether they were employees for a season or two, or if they are guests, short stay or long stay or coming back – we want to give that feeling of belonging and being yourself, because that was the freedom given to us.

I don't know if you'd call it a vision or a mission, and it's maybe a little bit corny, but we want it to be the best meeting place, because that's what people do at Trevarefabrikken. Yes, they have food, they see a concert, they have a beer, they go in the sauna, they swim, they explore the nature around – but all of those activities are tools to connect with people. That is Trevarefabrikken's project, but also its impact.

You have a lot of food and drink offerings at the factory – what would you say is the unifying element of all of them?

M: Our space can fit two hundred people inside downstairs, and two hundred outside. Especially in the summer season when it's warm, it's busy, there's sun, it's buzzing, so we're never going to be an a la carte restaurant or a fine dining restaurant; that's not us. It also wouldn't fit the community feeling.

It has to be somewhat easy, logistically, but it also has to reflect the values of Trevarefabrikken: authentic, honest, and local. That's the core. You can say what you want about another pizza place in Lofoten, but I think in some ways it's very authentic – it's something we deliberately have brought in because we like it. This year I'm very proud because we finally managed to incorporate a local ingredient on every pizza. The vegan pizza has seaweed; the spicy pepperoni now has nduja from a local farm; the four cheese has goat cheese from a local producer; the pesto on the Margherita is not basil pesto, but local wild garlic pesto. It's all these small things, which maybe in the big scheme don't matter, but which I feel are very important to be able to stay authentic and real, by using what's around us.

The same goes for our grill house that we finally opened this summer. Our grill chef Malin and I developed our fish burger, with local cod from Finnholmen in Henningsvær. Instead of using regular spices we use a seaweed spice mix from the girls at Lofoten Seaweed. And because you have to have fries when you have burgers, on our regular fries we incorporated another seaweed spice mix, so there's all these touches. Our Trevareburger uses smoked meat from a local farm up by Harstad/Narvik.

I think it is important to always try to use a local alternative and to have honest, good food. I'm not saying we're making the best burgers in the world – that's a very hard competition, and we're not only a burger place. We are a lot of things, but the things we do should be high quality, no matter if it's our homemade cinnamon buns or the almond croissants or our coffee (which is roasted locally). Maybe we'll even have our own roastery in the future.

And you've got your own beer too!

M: Yes, our very own Trevareøl is made by the local brewery Lofotpils in Svolvær. It is an unfiltered blonde ale, which in my opinion tastes like a sunny summer day in Henningsvær – perfect on our outdoor terrace.

I think that's pretty good going, you know.

M: I think so too. I often find it's easy to have this sense that it's never enough, but this year we've come a long way, even though it may not seem like it because it's still the same pizza house. If you take a close look at all the menus this year, though, I definitely feel we've done a Neil Armstrong for ourselves at least.

It's really impressive. It must be difficult to manage – café, bar, restaurant, sauna, wine bar, pizza oven, grill, yoga studio, festival?

M: I'm not going to say it's a monster, but it's really become an octopus in some ways, hasn't it?

It's a lifestyle more than a job.

M: Definitely. It really is. That's why we try to have some days every year where we don't actively work. Your brain is often on, but you also need that downtime to be able to develop. I think that is going to be important in the coming years to be able to sustain Trevarefabrikken, because we're on our tenth year.

Have you been able to find time to just sit and reflect on everything you've built together?

M: I have two favourite places to sit, actually. When you exit the wine bar, a lot of people often sit on that rock formation in the front or stand on the porch, but if you go directly to the right, there's this tiny little bench next to the old water tank and there, if you tuck into that corner, you'll have sun for many hours, that's one thing, but you will also be left alone because it's not so easy to see. That is my favourite spot. In summer when the wine bar is not open, I usually sit there because you're still close to everything, but you're also a little bit hidden.

And then, of course, there is this natural stone couch down by the sauna in the rock formation. It used to be a well-kept secret – not anymore – but you can still go there, have a swim, and be somewhat left alone.

There are a lot of hidden corners and details in the building dating back to when it was first built.

M: Yes. The floorboards you see when you're on the third floor looking up at the roof are wooden and they're the old wooden runway of Bodø Airport. The original electrical system actually comes from a sunken warship (Tirpitz) outside of Narvik during the Second World War, and the metal bearing in the concrete walls is originally German bunker armour. It's impressive how Alf Reidar reused stuff, he was really ahead of his time.

The whole place where Trevarefabrikken stands, there used to be water flowing through all of it, down to Joker, so it's actually an unnatural filling. It's been filled with stones and gravel.

Presumably by Alf Reidar.

M: Yes, and the hotel rooms have this brick flooring which are leftover bricks from the chimney. Same as the pizza oven, the oven itself is also made up of chimney bricks.

Then of course we have the liver pool behind the wine bar, and we're still talking about if that's going to be an actual pool at some point. It's the old original pool where all the cod liver got dumped before it went to steaming, and we're talking about making it into an actual modern pool with a glass roof so in winter you can float and look up at the Northern Lights. But we'll see if that actually happens.

You've got a lot of ambitions and a lot of dreams for the space.

M: There's still a lot to be done. We have a whole third floor to develop and a wine bar to finish. In ten years, there will probably still be something that's not done. I hope building-wise we're done, but you never know. There's this old material shed that used to be in the parking lot as well, that got torn down by a storm back in 2009. We're thinking maybe we should rebuild it. A lot of plans, always. So no kids anytime soon. Maybe a dog. Mats actually got a dog last year.

Do you see hope or excitement from the people of Henningsvær?

M: We see that now, the kids who grew up in Henningsvær, who used to want to get away, many of them have had summer jobs at Trevarefabrikken in the past. For instance, Cecilie, the local ceramicist, her son is studying in Bergen and her daughter is studying in The Hague, and now when people ask them where they're from, it's like, "I'm from Henningsvær," but they say it with pride.

Aligned

BY ANITA VALRYGG

I had had the place for a few years before I met Thomas. I dared to show him when we went out in an open boat on the coast of Helgeland, in March, six years ago. One of the walls had fallen during the winter storm, and I was afraid of what he would think of my project. Restoring a house on a deserted island, without electricity and water in North Norway, is no joke. And while I grew up near the Arctic Circle, Thomas was born in Paris. Perhaps I, who had grown up surrounded by nature at our weekend cabin, had my unconscious prejudices against a city boy?

When he and I arrived on the island, we were busy getting the building material we had brought with us safely ashore – and completely forgot that it was Good Friday, the longest tide of the year. It wasn't long before we found ourselves stranded; we had only planned to visit the island for a short trip and had neither water nor food with us. The next high tide that could lift the boat would come in twelve hours. A house without walls and windows in March – all we could do was carry the building materials we had brought with us to keep warm.

When Thomas caught sight of the house I held my breath, but he instinctively set to work just as I had done the first time I saw it. Time has taken its toll on the house. Trying to beat it is a losing battle, but one we pursued nonetheless.

Later that evening, when we had finally reached a warm cabin on the neighbouring island, Thomas sat down smiling, without saying a word. I almost didn't dare ask. Then he said, "I will spend everything I own and earn for the rest of my life on this place."

And that was it. North Norway was to become our next home.

—

During this time, we were living in Copenhagen, where I ran the architecture office VALRYGG studio, which I started ten years ago. Thomas was starting his business career in procurement, and life was exactly as it should be. But the little house on the island called to us; we were left missing the summer in mild Helgeland and just wanted to spend all our free time on our project. Flying north from Copenhagen on weekends went against our desire for a smaller carbon footprint, so we moved north to be closer to the island. This would give us more time to repair the urgent holes in the walls and roof, and to restore and replace the blown out windows and doors before the winter weather could take it away from us forever.

At home in the North, winter welcomed us in its own way. It's something you have to feel in your body to understand. We quickly realised that the island could not be our only home, due to the storms and isolation, and began to look for a place that was easier to live in all year round. We found a small farm on a not-quite-deserted island, Handesøya, Nesna municipality, where the population is only sixty people. We now commute between the two islands.

At our farm in Handesøya we have everything we need – water from our own source, a forest whose wood warms us and has allowed us to build the vegetable garden. The island is located in the innermost fjord of the islands on Helgeland, and we have mountains and the sea to forage from. We live on the south side, with hot summers and therefore a good season to grow vegetables and berries. Being able to harvest straight from nature is something I've done since childhood, but I am still surprised by how much we can eat from the wild plants around us – dandelion, among many other plants, as wild salads and in stews; seaweed pasta; Fireweed "asparagus"; birch sap and pine syrup, as well as blueberry jam and cloudberries, which have long traditions in the Arctic. Many of the plants we see as weeds, like Lady's Mantle and Ground Elder, are perfect for making into pesto, and full of vitamins and minerals. Some of this knowledge has been forgotten, which is why I persistently try to absorb it and to pass it on.

—

For over ten years I worked from Copenhagen on architectural projects in Helgeland and Lofoten. Now that I live here, my role has changed with our life; I work more holistically with the projects and often spend long periods of time in the same place. I go into the local communities and get to know the people who live there. The buildings must give something of themselves to those who live in and around them, and my architecture has helped to create an identity for places in North Norway. My desire is to bring urban qualities to small towns with the help of unexpected buildings far out in the sea gap.

One of these is the newly opened Lovund Boat Museum in Helgeland, which floats over the water and welcomes you when you arrive. Central to the museum is the remains of a boat from circa 1460 which was found at the site – the only boat from the Middle Ages that has been found and preserved in the region. The boat connects Lovund with the past, and with other regions and nations. Embracing the remains, the museum appears to levitate, with only a few pillars to hold it aloft. Changing expression in step with the tides, the building sometimes almost floats on the water, while at other times you can walk under it on the rocky shores below. The construction also allows light to enter under the building in order to sustain life on the shore, and the light from the waves is reflected up and into the exhibition room, the shadows imitating the movement of the sea. Overhead, the protective brick roof mimics those of the rusty boathouses traditional in the coastal cultural landscape. The project has brought together many exciting people from various fields over several years, including the children on the island, who have collected stones from the shore to put under the boat.

I feel increasingly strongly that my role in this society is about sharing my own inspiration in order to inspire others, and being creative in so many more ways than I could ever imagine. I have spent the last two years observing, and drawing from all the raw materials we have in nature and the eternal change through the seasons. I learn new plant species and processes in nature, and I see connections of which I have not previously been aware. Whereas in the city I worked with shapes on a computer screen, I now also work with seasonal growth, structures, and colours, and I am convinced that this makes me a better architect. Now I work on projects that challenge the way we live and how we can become more aware of the resources around us; I design vegetable gardens and saunas, oversee the transformation of barns, and develop locally produced travel souvenirs together with craftsmen in the region.

—

Running an architectural office, building up a small farm, and restoring a house on a deserted island never gets boring. Meanwhile, Thomas is starting a bakery here on Handesøya and has started delivering the post. Although we live on a small island, it's quite busy and it never gets boring in this small community. We have learned to take the time to notice the bustling natural life that surrounds us throughout the seasons and all the opportunities that exist as soon as we step off the asphalt and onto the grass.

The seasons in the North are full of contrasts, but it is the countless transitions that are exciting; from gathering truffle seaweed in February, to bottling birch sap in April, and then there are rowan leaf sprouts and fir shoots, wild lettuce in the garden, and an abundance of berries throughout the autumn. How do we take care of all this? As an architect, this is something I want to continue to consider: how do we organise our homes and local environment to take care of everything we have around us? How can we collect directly from nature, and what we can grow to be as self-sufficient as possible here in the North?

To be so closely in touch with nature that you can lie on the forest floor and study it – it's a feeling you can't shake off. Although our journey took us from Los Angeles to Copenhagen and beyond, nature has always had a place in my architecture and creativity – like a distant call from the North which kept getting louder.

We commute six months out of the year between the house on the deserted island and the farm on Handesøya. Because the short summer season here is almost explosive, with twenty four hours of daylight, we have to keep an eye on the vegetable garden on the farm. We are visited by friends from all over the world who may have never before caught the fish they are going to eat, or gathered live scallops and crabs, or even used a very basic outdoor toilet, for that matter.

While we may not have running water, we have the sea, which gives us most of what we need. Here there are white beaches and coves where we can swim, and only a few trees that have barely managed to stretch a metre above the ground. It's windy and magical. The sky on the island is huge, and it changes all the time, like the colours of the heather and the grass. It's always exciting to arrive for the first time after the long winter has let go, because we never know what we will get.

The sea is rising and the storms are getting stronger every year, but the work we have done with the house means that we can be a little less anxious every winter. The next task is to restore the boathouse – I dream of a sauna there, and to lay an anchor for a sailboat so that friends along the coast can more easily come and visit us.

—

Like the two islands that comprise Henningsvær, the "mainland" of Lofoten's archipelago is itself three islands – Moskenesøya, Vestvågsøya, and Austvågsøya. Austvågsøya is connected by bridge with the island of Hinnøya, from which Lofoten stretches northwards into Vesterålen, an altogether separate archipelago, which shares in the drama of Lofoten's scenery but without (as of yet) the same buzz or reputation.

The road into Vesterålen follows a winding scenic route along the water. There we stayed in a beautiful old wooden home, painted a deep blue, in a tiny village called Blokken. We were here for the first time to visit a friend of ours, Halvar Ellingsen, who we'd met years before down south in Mosjøen. Now, having moved up to Vesterålen with his family, he was running a restaurant and farm called Kvitnes Gård.

In the morning, before we drove to Kvitnes, we sat out on the porch of our blue house in wool jumpers and thick socks, sipping hot drinks as we faced out to sea, charmed by complete silence and cloudless skies.

Kvitnes Gård

Several years ago, an unexpected phone call drew Chef Halvar Ellingsen from the orbit of Michelin-starred restaurants in Oslo to a small fjord-side farm in remote Vesterålen. Halvar had been offered a chance few chefs could turn down: the opportunity to create his own farm-led restaurant on a historic steading that stretches across fields, through forests, and down to the rocky beaches of the fjord. The setting seemed postcard-perfect.

The name of the farm, Kvitnes, wasn't one which had significance to Halvar. But he would be made to remember it, later on, when he shared the news with his family: "Kvitnes?" his father chimed in, "How could you forget the name of the Ellingsen family farm? The farm your great-great-great-grandfather built!" Stunned, suddenly Halvar's chance opportunity became something more like a fateful reunion.

Though once the Ellingsen family farm, it hadn't been for quite some time, and in the intervening years, over the course of multiple ownerships, Kvitnes Gård had fallen on hard times. When it was purchased in 2012 by Helge Mørck it was in desperate need of extensive renovation and repair, yet the core of the farm, with its historic home and many of its old outbuildings, were still intact. With Mørck's help, Halvar began a slow process of renewal – stripping down some dilapidated and disused buildings, and gutting and refitting others.

It took several years to fully restore the farm: a process which, from an agricultural perspective, included tending to and rejuvenating local soil health, the installation of a large greenhouse and dozens of raised beds, the planting of thousands of vegetables, fruits, and herbs suited to the tough Arctic conditions, and the purchase and rearing of well over a hundred animals (pigs, rabbits, goats, sheep, chickens, and quails, among others). When all was said and done, Halvar had recruited a team of gardeners, chefs, waiters, and sommeliers, created prep and restaurant kitchens, as well as a dining space, to rival anywhere in the Nordic region.

In many ways, the scope and success of Kvitnes Gård is a subversion of popular opinion – and the notion that the Arctic cannot sustain a local culinary experience which is at once founded in heritage whilst also exploring depth and diversity. As a dining experience, it is frequently counted amongst the best in Norway if not the entire Nordic region, yet what is even more incredible is that the Kvitnes Gård team has not sacrificed their culinary ambitions in their pursuit of self-sufficiency. In fact, by tapping into local knowledge and traditional practice, they have been able to create a menu using only their own vegetables and produce – fresh, preserved, or fermented. This is a stunning show of the strength of the local ecosystems and encapsulates a holistic experience which is a tribute to the landscape and respectful nurturing of its potential. For Halvar and his team, it is a bold and also beautiful "homecoming."

LEFT: *Villsau* ("wild sheep"), a heritage breed of Norwegian sheep, which is one of the oldest in Europe.

Sheep skins are salted (to prevent bacteria)
before being used as cushioning in the restaurant.

Ox-blood red is perhaps the most iconic colour for traditional-style wooden buildings in Norway. This is due to the fact that historically, the iron oxide used as pigment (a by-product of copper mining) was low-cost. Other pigments, and by extension, paints, were much more expensive to source and produce, and thus became a status symbol for the well-to-do. Blue is one of those colours.

LEFT: Sourdough toast brushed with fermented garlic syrup and topped with whale (meat from a marbled section, located just before the tail), and cured fat from Kvitnes Gård Mangalitsa pigs. This cut of whale is rarely, if ever, used in Norway — but is prized abroad, especially in Japanese cuisine.

BELOW: *Goro* (a thin traditional Norwegian cake/cracker) filled with brown cheese and cloudberries.

RIGHT: Halibut aged for three weeks, which is salted for two hours, and then grilled with hay for five minutes. Served with almost burnt butter, almost burnt cream, and fermented mackerel.

LEFT: Blood pancake (made using sheep blood) filled with black currants, salted leg of lamb (*fenalår*) powder and a cream made of roses; served with a sorbet made of goat yoghurt, meadowsweet and spruce shoot.

I first met Máret on a boat sailing into Norway's northernmost waters. The boat was part of the Hurtigruten fleet of ships which were once essential lifelines for Norwegian villages in the Arctic, bringing mail and medicine to remote communities, but which today functions more like a cruise ship, providing transport for people and goods along the coast.

As part of a special onboard event, Máret was presenting a talk to a small crowded theatre on her lifestyle and practices as a proud Sámi, cultural activist, and reindeer herder. Afterwards, I was able to meet with her and spend time together one-on-one. We spoke about our project and how eager we were to learn more about Sámi culture as well as the modern realities and adaptations of their otherwise traditional lifestyle.

Máret, a generous host, invited us to her hometown, Kautokeino ("Guovdageaidnu" in Northern Sámi), where she was en route to visit her parents. We graciously accepted, and experienced a singularly unforgettable introduction into the heart of Sámi culture in North Norway. We would return to visit Máret throughout the seasons, each time at her family home in Ofoten, a fjord-side municipality just east of Lofoten. During each visit, we were able to get a better understanding of her way of life, and her insights as an individual.

It is hard not to be moved by Máret; hard not to have your perspectives challenged or changed, and your body, heartbeat, or even internal voice settle into a rhythm that opens up your senses and attunes you with your immediate surroundings.

The Reindeer and the Sámi

AS TOLD BY MÁRET RÁVDNÁ BULJO

There is a legend from a long time ago, when the animals could speak and the people understood the language of animals.

One winter the reindeer were struggling because, as it often was, there were so many wolves and they were always hungry. The reindeer were tired of this. When the reindeer tried to dig down to the ground to find food, the wolves would come and hunt them, so the reindeer had to run and didn't have enough time to eat.

On one nice day the reindeer heard the wolves coming, but the wolves didn't chase them. The wolves were being chased by humans. And the reindeer realised that there was an opportunity for another way of living, because the wolves also had enemies they were afraid of.

The reindeer spoke to each other and decided to contact the humans. So the reindeer went to the Sámi people and said, "We see that you are chasing the wolves and the wolves are afraid of you. We are afraid of the wolves and we never get enough time to eat, so we are starving. We see that the wolves are afraid of you, so we were thinking about making you a deal. The wolves come to us. If you watch over us when we are eating you will get the wolves easily and we will have more peace to eat." The Sámi thought it was a good idea.

So they started to watch over the reindeer and the wolves came. The humans could hunt the wolves. And the reindeer said, "We don't want you to do this for free. You need food. You need fur for your clothing, and antlers and bones for your tools. We will offer you ourselves as payment if you continue to watch over us. You will get what you need, not more or less, only what you need, but you have to promise that you use every part of the reindeer for something useful – don't waste anything. Then you will live well and we will live well."

So they made this pact, and since that day the reindeer and the Sámi have worked and lived together.

Máret Rávdná Buljo

Máret comes from a long line of reindeer herders that stretches back to a time long before distinct national borders, when nomadic Sámi people ranged freely through their homeland (Sápmi), an area which stretched across four countries (Norway, Sweden, Finland, and Russia) and saw the frequent migration of families, communities, and animals from mountains to pasture or grazing land throughout the year.

While not all Sámi come from reindeer herding backgrounds (some, called "Coastal Sámi," live more of their lives by the water), it is arguably the oldest active lifestyle in North Norway. They are one of the few Indigenous peoples in Europe, and the only amongst the northernmost regions of Fennoscandia, however they have experienced centuries of persecution and prejudice by foreigners and – especially in the last couple hundred years – the Norwegian government, which organised programmes of Christianisation, forced relocation, and state schooling that were meant to integrate them firmly into a more homogenised Norwegian society.

Today, thankfully, there is much greater acceptance and celebration of Sámi people and cultures, though some Sámi may still face prejudice and racism in today's society, and it can at times be an up-hill battle to maintain, rediscover, and reinvigorate communities and aspects of culture which were systemically erased.

Enter into this fight Máret Rávdná Buljo, who, alongside her husband Peder Ingar Hansen Buljo (a native of Lofoten, who hails from one of the area's last native Sámi herding families) fights to honour and preserve Sámi heritage in its full richness and depth. In the process, she seeks out the voice and the memories of her ancestors, and draws inspiration from the way they saw their place in the natural world.

Ben Mervis with Máret Rávdná Buljo

Could you share with me your journey and memories of the connection with reindeer and how that began for you?

MÁRET: My first memory of a reindeer was when I was lying in the sled during the spring migration, and this reindeer with big antlers came and looked down at me. That was my first fascination with reindeer. And I fell in love with reindeer then, because of this encounter. I was three years old, and that's my first memory.

What you described almost has a paternal or maternal quality to it, with the reindeer looking over you as you're young.

M: Yeah, it was, I felt it was a kind of protection too, even though he had these big antlers. But I think – since I remember it so well – I was quite scared too. It's burned into my mind.

That connection, was it something that your parents actively nurtured, or it just kind of grew organically for you?

M: My parents always wanted us to continue with the reindeer herding. It's our job. It's our lifestyle. It's what we are meant to do on this Earth. We can't imagine another life. And even with all the opposition we've faced, we still continue fighting for our home, our life. Our role is to fight, to take care of the reindeer in this area. We've never dreamt about another life. It's here where we are supposed to be and live.

There is a legend from a long time ago, when the Sámi and the reindeer made a pact to work together, and that's why we are still following the reindeer today. We don't have the wolves anymore, as they had, but we have other kinds of wolves today. Instead we have big industry taking our land, we are losing land all the time, and we are fighting. I've been fighting against the wolves so they don't eat our reindeer. So the work continues, and we still get meat from the reindeer.

Can you talk more about the kind of modern-day wolves that would take away from the land and change the way of living?

M: You are afraid every day, you're always anxious about losing land. It's very worrying, people poisoning the air, poisoning the water, poisoning the Earth. It's terrifying, and sometimes I feel helpless. We have a responsibility to take care of the land so that we can continue to have clean water and clean air. And it seems like the rest of the world doesn't understand. The Earth is just seen as money. People are not thinking, "What about the fifty thousand other years?" We are going to use up these resources in two hundred years or less, like the wolves just eating and eating and eating and not thinking about what we are taking, and that it could disappear.

I think in our world today, there's a lot about getting the most out of something or getting something quickly.

M: Yes. When I am harvesting from nature, I'm also thinking "I need clean water for this to grow. I need to protect this lake, this river, this land where the cloudberries grow, and where the reindeer are grazing, or the moose, or where the birds are building their nests." I take what is necessary, but I don't take everything. You have to know when to stop, what to leave. Don't take all the cloudberries you find, continue to another spot and always leave some to grow for next season. Also with fishing, you don't take more than what you need. And if you get a lot of fish, you share with your family.

And are those values that you feel were taught to you as a kid growing up? Or they've just always been there and you don't know where they came from?

M: Kids at school used to say, "You are so poor. You always have this dry reindeer meat on your bread. You can't buy salami because you are so poor. You are using this reindeer skin hat because you can't afford [anything else]." But at home, I always heard, "When you are wearing this, you are honouring our lifestyle. Thank you." And also, eating reindeer meat means that you are honouring the reindeer. That was what I heard at home. So I was silent about it [at school], and I stood out.

Do you still experience people looking down on the Sámi?

M: Yeah, a lot. For example, because I don't want to build a brand-new house. The luxury of today is time, it's freedom to take the time. I'm attracted to people who think in the same way as me, and are part of this community – you need it so you don't feel alone. It doesn't need to be Sámi people that I am connected to, but people all around the world who are on the same track, taking care of the land. Even when you have this modern life, you can do it another way that is softer for nature, you can take care of nature instead of destroying it.

Could you talk me through a year of living with reindeer and how that year progresses and evolves?

M: Reindeer year begins on the first of May, and on the third day in May, it is the *Ruos'mes'beaivi*, the day of reindeer calves. And depending on the weather that day, you can tell what the weather will be like through the first month in the calf's life. For example, if the weather is wet on that day, it will be a very good spring, and the snow will melt easily, and it will be very green early. But if it is very cold and frosty on that day, that kind of weather will continue for a month, and it's not so good for newborn reindeer calves.

And then you have other days too, like when the bear wakes from hibernation, and when the new leaves come. The reindeer migrate on instinct, but we follow them to make sure they go to the right place, because reindeer are curious, especially the young reindeer. But every reindeer has in their cells the memory of where their ancestors went, so they are programmed where to go, even the young ones who have lost their mother. They know which direction they are supposed to go. It's very fascinating.

It's interesting that you bring up the ancestors of the reindeer, because I remember you talking often also about the connection that you have with your ancestors. It seems that both the reindeer and the Sámi people are living with that deep connection to the past, and the instinct that comes from ancestry.

M: Yeah, it's in our bloodstream; you just know. Even knowledge about nature. It is there; even if you have lost it, you can take it back, but you need to listen and you need to make your body available to reach this knowledge. It's timeless.

We are always watching the reindeer. When do the antlers start growing? Who will lose the antlers first, and why? And also, who needs to continue having antlers until the spring? Because they need this weapon to find food. And also the females who are carrying new life – she keeps her antlers longest, because she needs to have this weapon on her head because she is eating for two. The biggest male reindeer lose their antlers early, before Christmas. During the wintertime, their job is to protect. When he finds food and starts eating, the female comes and pushes him away with her antlers. He is a gentleman, so he will go and dig another hole for himself to eat. That is how it works with reindeer during wintertime. And in the summer and autumn, he grows new antlers – very big antlers. In the summer [the reindeer] go back up to the highest points of the mountains, to get away from the heat and the insects. When they are there, without trees, the antlers of the male reindeer are like the forest, so it's not as easy for the eagles to take calves, because [the males] are protecting them.

And you would slaughter the reindeer in autumn, or just before winter?

M: In our philosophy, we slaughter the reindeer who we know cannot survive the winter. We can read it on them: how their antlers have grown, how their fur looks, if there are any abnormalities. Then we know this reindeer might die during winter. Our job is to take out those reindeer that don't fit in, to keep the reindeer herd healthy and synchronised with each other during wintertime.

In the Sámi philosophy, you don't slaughter reindeer calves as your main slaughter animal. Because the mothers will cry. You don't want all your reindeer herd in sorrow because of you. So we slaughter in autumn before they go into the mating time. And mostly we slaughter big male reindeer, not all of them but some of them, for food, and we also sell the meat.

What are the first things you would make with the reindeer meat or blood, some of the traditional Sámi foods that would start to be prepared when you slaughter the reindeer?

M: The first reindeer slaughter in the new year is very sacred. Also to honour the sun coming back, and also the fish. The first cloudberries, you always share that food. If you eat alone, then you'll lose many; it's a sign of losing people around you. So you are scared to eat alone, if you are not sharing. Even with a guest who comes to visit you, you share everything you have.

When we slaughter reindeer, one of the first things we make is blood sausages. We clean the intestines and then we put the blood inside, and we boil it with meat. To get the broth for blood sausages, we boil the reindeer backbones. And we also use that as fresh meat for the family. There are some rules, like which part of the back is for women. The tail is for the one who slaughtered the reindeer, as a payment. There are also parts for the men who are growing big muscles, and parts for the teenagers. And then you have the youngest ones, they need to grow muscles, but in a softer way. So there are rules on how to slice backbones. This is the holy meal, the first meal from a reindeer. It's very sacred.

You've spoken [in the past] about this reindeer soul, the three souls of the reindeer, and I was wondering if you could tell me about that?

M: Yeah. There are three parts of a reindeer that keep a reindeer alive. A reindeer needs the brain – consciousness to know where to find food, where to go, what is the danger. Then the reindeer needs the bloodstream, the heart, to keep the body moving. The third one is the skin and the meat, the muscles, to keep the body together. Every part needs each other. And if you take one part off, then the body will not survive.

When we slaughter a reindeer, we have a moment of silence when they are between life and death, so they can pass peacefully. Once they have passed, the first symbol of death we make is for the skin and the meat, a cross on the chest, the symbol to bring the skin and the meat to death. This is, of course, after the reindeer is dead. Then you come to the heart, and you make this cross, and you cut the heart to bring out the blood inside. It's also a symbol to bring the heart and blood over to death, so you can eat in good conscience.

The last part is to make this cross under the head, the skull of the reindeer, to allow the consciousness to cross over. And after that, you can start eating the reindeer. You have brought the reindeer to the other side.

And afterwards when you are finished eating the reindeer, you put the bones back in nature, because it will bring back a new reindeer or many reindeer.

And how important is preservation, like salting or pickling or jamming?

M: It's very important. Of course, today we have freezers and many of the culture's preserving methods have been lost. But I am trying to bring back these old traditions, trying to figure out how they did it. When they didn't have a lot of salt for the yeast, how did they make the yeast to preserve the meat? When they didn't have sugar, where can I find sugar in nature? There was one woman who said, you watch the birds, you watch the animals, especially predators, how they preserve the food when they are hiding meat.

And not just food. You can study the birds, how they make their nests, so your feet don't freeze. So inside our gáma, our footwear, we put grass. Then you won't freeze. Studying nature – that is how you can survive.

Can you share a bit about the work that you do as a researcher?

M: I don't get paid for this. That's important. I do this as my lifestyle. It's my life and what I will bring to my children and hopefully they will remember when they grow older. We have been through a very long history, many hundreds of years of being forced to forget about our spiritual contact with food, with nature, because people were afraid. It was like a witch hunt for centuries, and people were killed if the government discovered they were doing what they thought was witchcraft. And there's also a long history of Norwegianising our people, forcing them to be more Norwegian and forget about the Sámi culture, taking kids away from home, putting them in a school where they only have Norwegians to take care of them. And so the kids lost the knowledge – this was in my parent's generation. I think my parents were very lucky that they had strong women who took care of the kids. When school was over, they took the kids up to the mountains, and they lived with the reindeer. So I am from a family that has been teaching the children to take care of the traditional knowledge, and appreciating its value outside of capitalism.

You are rich when you are able to live without money. I have been reading books by the priests when they came into Sápmi and were observing the Sámi. Often, the Sámi are [described as] wild people and poor, having to make flour from the bark of trees because they don't have wheat. But for me, if I read a sentence like that, I want to know about the flour they made. So I go to the elders and ask, "Do you remember how to make flour from bark and how to use it?" Some elders are very ashamed, because it was when they were so poor. "You don't need that anymore." But then I ask someone else who tells me how they made it, and why. You need that part from the trees, because it's a hard winter. You need energy. You need to walk and you don't want to carry heavy food. Then this bread is genius, because it's light and gives you a lot of energy.

Yeah, it's really fascinating to me because from what I read, the Sámi traditions were mostly oral and not about carrying around big books that you had to read through; how smart and how instinctive and sharp the Sámi people need to be to inherit this wisdom and then pass it on to the next generation. It's immense.

M: Yeah. Today, I'm very afraid of losing the knowledge, of losing the oral way of passing knowledge to each other. Because you can't keep it only in your head. You need to print; print with your footsteps and with your hands. If you continue doing the work with your hands, walking the land with your feet, then you will get the knowledge up to your head. But if you stop using your hands, then you only have a little bit in your head, not the full knowledge. For instance, I had heard a lot about reindeer milking, but my parents were kids when they stopped milking the reindeer. I have been longing for the reindeer milk, I wanted to know how it tastes, how I can make food with it – cheese, yoghurt, and preserve the milk. I decided I had to learn to do it; I had to get the knowledge into my fingertips. So I started to keep the reindeer with me to get them very tame, and last year I started to milk one reindeer. I didn't know how. I read about milking in books, but they don't explain how to do it. How you hold your fingers, how the reindeer will react, how the reindeer will stand. You can't find that in books, you have to experience it. My biggest teacher with the milking has been the reindeer herself. But I have also used very old techniques, like reindeer whispering, to communicate with the reindeer in a spiritual way. I know it works. It's amazing.

It's been tears of sorrow, tears of the pain my people have been through, because of the lost knowledge about reindeer milking, it's been tears for the reindeer. And it's been tears full of joy, full of love for the reindeer and also the love of connection. Now I'm able to connect with the reindeer and I have seen the reindeer with new eyes because of that, because I have experienced the milking for myself. It's so high value for me and I have learned so much, and that's something I want to continue with.

And also seeing the joy in my children's eyes when they taste the milk for the first time, and also joy in my parent's eyes because they haven't tasted the milk for fifty years and now I'm bringing it back. My children were really glad when I made the yoghurt. We ate that with some fermented cloudberries. That is a taste that you can't find in any restaurants. It's like melted ice cream, very good ice cream. But I have also met experienced Sámi reindeer herders who were very afraid of tasting the reindeer milk; they couldn't do it. And there are reindeer people who can't eat reindeer brain, because they think it's nasty or dirty. But of course I understand our people have been told that this kind of food is for poor people. We've been told to only eat the fillet, like rich men. But I have learned to not care about others, what they say, or how they see us. You have the right to live as you are. The value of the reindeer, that is the most important. The reindeer appreciates you, and feeling the love from the reindeer that you are doing the right thing – that is the most valuable.

Restaurants are also able to work with the milk and put it on the table as this gourmet food. Then I see the value of my work. That is the payment for my work, to see this joy in people's eyes. I saw the love and the tears for what is lost. And also the tears of hope. It's been a very deep journey for me. I didn't earn any money for that. I am rich inside myself, from the experience.

Which are some of the places that you work with locally?

M: I prefer to choose customers who have the same values about food as I have. We want to sell our reindeer meat to people who are telling our story. Locally, for example, a restaurant nearby is very highly rated, Kvitnes Gård. Their philosophy is from the earth to the table; this connection with nature.

And then I also sell reindeer meat to Sámi people, especially elders, and that is so valuable for me when Sámi elders come to us and say, "You have the right taste of reindeer meat, what we remember when we were children. You are not doing industrial things and we have been searching for this taste and you have it, you still have it, and I don't care how much it costs, I will have it." Because what it contains is the philosophy. That is confirmation for me that I'm doing the right thing, continuing to do it better and spread the word.

It must be very gratifying to bring that joy and memory to the elders.

M: I'm always thinking, "What would my grandmother say? What would she be grateful for and be happy for?"

I have said no to things that are not good for my reindeer. For example, we have bought a property here that was a camping site before. There used to be a lot of tourists around, but we shut it down. We could charge a lot of money to feed the reindeer, or drive with a reindeer. But I didn't want my reindeer to be tourist reindeer and pulling a sled all day or eating more and more because it pleases the tourists. If you give too much food to a reindeer it disturbs the biology inside their stomach, and then you are destroying the reindeer. So I didn't want that. We could make a lot of money, but I prefer not to.

We also use modern technology to take care of people and nature. Like instead of using a snowmobile, we can use a drone and so we are not touching the ground as much. We also have GPS trackers on some reindeer, so we know where they are. I can sleep well now. Even when we are not with the reindeer all the time. Taking care of my mental health is very necessary, so I can sleep well. With the GPS, I know the reindeer are not close to the road or in the village.

There's something that I think is very beautiful that keeps coming up in our conversation, which I think is synchronicity, and not just with nature and with the reindeer. Just living in a way which is kind of patient and observant and respectful.

M: Yeah, this is the goal to reach. It also reminds you of your role on this Earth. What is your role? To take care, to synchronise all the things – that is your work. You, as a human, with your hands and with your brain, can do something. You need to get the sign from nature, the call. Then, with the spiritual work, you know what to do. But, of course, today, with the states and laws and everything, we are forbidden to do our traditional work, to bring nature into balance.

I suppose that's where your work comes in. You know, trying to bring that balance.

M: Yeah, to know my place. That's my work.

Máret is especially interested in traditional Sámi foods, including those which are fading out of memory. Here she forages for pine bark, which is cleaned and baked before being blitzed in a blender and mixed with fat (in this case, reindeer brain) to form a nutrient-rich thin bread or cracker.

The Living

The blood pancake is a staple of traditional Sámi home cooking: this version is a favourite of her sons. It uses wheat flour and is slightly sweetened — like a crêpe — and topped here with yoghurt, cloudberries, and honey.

RIGHT: Three generations of the same family: Máret Rávdná Buljo, her niece Elle Májja Eira, and her mother Karen Marie Eira Buljo.

Dried reindeer meat fills the belly for long hikes up the mountain. Máret and her son Jusse Niklas are waiting for signs of her family's herd, slowly trekking over the mountain.

The Living

The use of modern technology allows Sámi reindeer herders to make less of a footprint on the mountain. Máret's son Peder Issát is adept at flying drones to monitor the progress of the herd.

Máret Rávdná Buljo

The bond Máret maintains with her reindeer reflects that of mother and child. This embrace is a gesture of vulnerability amongst the reindeer, demonstrating the special trust that exists between Máret and her herd.

Máret Rávdná Buljo

The taste of reindeer-milk had almost fallen out of memory in Norway before Máret began to rediscover these lost techniques. The reindeer are especially finicky and tough to milk, but through patience and by sensing the reindeers' response, Máret has been able to revive the tradition, even making reindeer-milk yoghurt and cottage cheese.

Much like the prow of a ship, Sámi boots are curved at the toe to prevent snow from falling back over the wearer's foot, keeping them warmer for longer.

Máret Rávdná Buljo

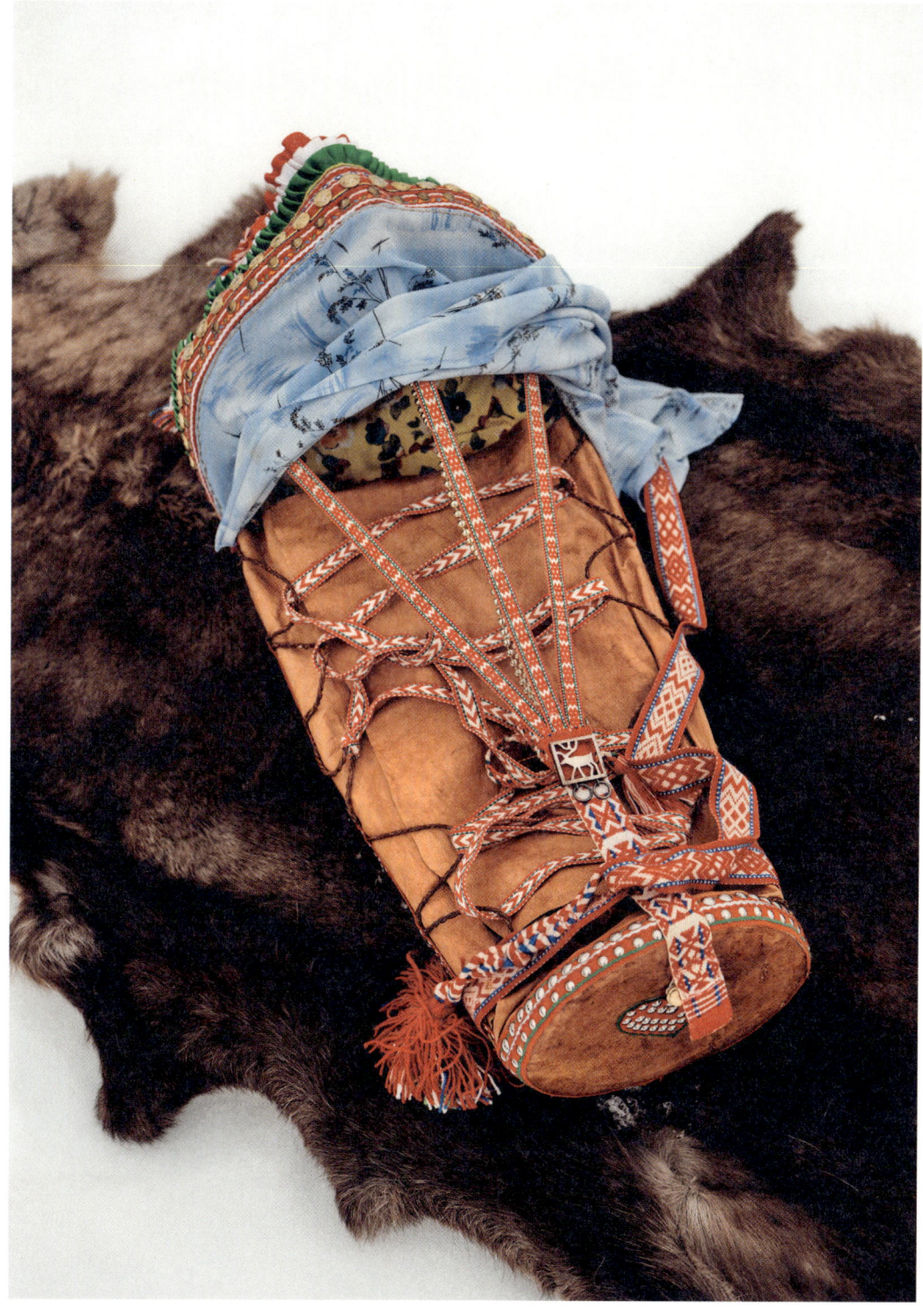

A traditional wooden Sámi cradle with straps woven by Máret's mother, which has held both Máret and her siblings, as well as her own sons. In days long past, as Sámi travelled with their families, the cradle would be hung from the back of the tamest reindeer — the gentle rhythm of the movement rocking the infant and keeping them calm.

Childhood Memory of Nordland

Oh, I know of a land

Far up north so adored,

With a shore of white sand

Between mountains and fjord.

Where I'm welcome as a son,

Where my heartstrings are spun

With the silkiest, silkiest strand:

I remember, remember so dearly this land!

FROM *CHILDHOOD MEMORY OF NORDLAND* BY ELIAS BLIX
TRANSLATED BY FINN TØMMERBERG

Barndomsminne frå Nordland

Å eg veit meg eit land
langt der oppe mot nord,
med ei lysande strand
mellom høgfjell og fjord.
Der eg gjerne er gjest,
der mitt hjarta er fest
med dei finaste, finaste band.
Å eg minnest, eg minnest så vel dette land!

FRA BARNDOMSMINNE FRÅ NORDLAND AV ELIAS BLIX

This book is the culmination of several trips through Norway, and only made possible due to the incredible generosity of the people who live there – who helped guide our way throughout the seasons.

So many people have helped shape our path, and we want to say a special thank you to the following:

Alf Martinsen
Alf Per Johansen
Anine Hansen
Anita Valrygg
Anniken Zahl Furunes
ArktiskMat
Bodø 2024
Åshild Blyseth
Dagrunn Grønbech
Einar Niemi
Eric Ryan
Espen Reines
Gadus Norway
Finn Tømmerberg
Guro Larsen Brown
Halvar Ellingsen
Håvard Ånensen
Ingrid Erøy
Jason Ball
Karen Marie Eira Buljo
Katrine Remmen Wiken

Marianne Myrnes Steinrud
Martin Hjelle
Mats Alfsen
Máret Rávdná Buljo
Marte Ryan
NordNorsk Reiseliv AS
Nordnorsk Kompetansesenter MAT
Peder Ingar Buljo
Per Einar Steinrud
Per Theodor Tørrissen
Remi Fagervik
Roderick Sloan
Runar Hestmark
Samfunnsløftet Sparebank 1 Nord-Norge
Sara Ellen Anne Buljo Eira
Trond Lysholm

EDITOR
Ben Mervis

SUB-EDITORS
Kenzie Yoshimura
Anna Moore

PHOTOGRAPHY
Liz Seabrook

ILLUSTRATIONS
Anine Hansen

CREATIVE DIRECTOR
Ric Bell

ART DIRECTION & DESIGN
POST – deliveredbypost.com

GRAPHIC DESIGNER
Dylan Reilly

PRINT
KOPA

TYPEFACES
Rhetorik (AllCaps)
Dia (Schick Toikka)

A CIP catalogue record for this book is available from the British Library

ISBN
978-1-0369-0081-6

First published in the United Kingdom in 2024 by Fare Folk Ltd

Flat 1, 595 Shields Road,
Glasgow, G41 2RW

fare-folk.com

Copyright © Fare Folk Ltd

The moral right of the author has been asserted.

All Rights Reserved. No part of this publication may be reproduced or transmitted in any form or by any means, electronic or mechanical, including photocopy, recording, or any other information storage and retrieval system, without prior written consent from the publisher.

All photographs and illustration material is the copyright property of the artists and/or their estates. Every effort has been made to contact and properly credit copyright holders. Please contact us regarding corrections or omissions.

Please note interviews included within are edited for clarity and length.